Martha Frances

To Martha;
Thank you for
your work of
reconciliation.

9-26-06

THE
CHURCH
ENSLAVED

"**A book that dares to say what must be said.** It raises the right questions, offers an excellent section on American culture from an African perspective, and is a wonderful resource for group studies."

–John T. Galloway Jr.,
Pastor, Wayne Presbyterian Church,
Author of *Ministry Loves Company*

OTHER TITLES IN

PRISMS

Turn Your Church Inside Out:
Building a Community for Others
Walt Kallestad

A Servant's Manual:
Christian Leadership for Tomorrow
Michael W. Foss

Spiritual Maturity:
Preserving Congregational Health and Balance
Frank A. Thomas

Moving beyond Church Growth:
An Alternative Vision for Congregations
Mark A. Olson

Beyond the Scandals:
A Guide to Healthy Sexuality for Clergy
G. Lloyd Rediger

Healing Bodies and Souls:
A Practical Guide for Congregations
W. Daniel Hale and Harold G.Koenig

The Right Road:
Life Choices for Clergy
Gwen Wagstrom Halaas

THE
CHURCH
ENSLAVED

A Spirituality of
Racial Reconciliation

Tony Campolo
and
Michael Battle

Fortress Press
Minneapolis

THE CHURCH ENSLAVED
A Spirituality of Racial Reconciliation
Prisms Series

Scripture quotations, unless otherwise noted, are from the New Revised Standard Version (NRSV) Bible, copyright © 1989 Division of Christian Education of the National Council of Churches of Christ in the United States of America. Used by permission.

Cover photo © Bob Elsdale/The Image Bank/Getty Images. Used by permission.
Cover design: Laurie Ingram
Book design: James Korsmo

Library of Congress Cataloging-in-Publication Data
Campolo, Anthony.
  The church enslaved : a spirituality of racial reconciliation / Tony Campolo and Michael Battle.
      p. cm. — (Prisms)
  Includes bibliographical references (p.   ).
  ISBN 0-8006-3697-X (alk. paper)
  1. Race relations—Religious aspects—Christianity. 2. Reconciliation—Religious aspects—Christianity. 3. Church. I. Battle, Michael, 1963- II. Title. III. Series.
  BT734.2.C27 2005
  277.3'083'089—dc22   2005008380

The paper used in this publication meets the minimum requirements of American National Standard for Information Sciences — Permanence of Paper for Printed Library Materials, ANSI Z329.48-1984.

Manufactured in the U.S.A.

09   08   07   06   05   1   2   3   4   5   6   7   8   9   10

CONTENTS

PREFACE

W e invite you to journey with us into the core of "America's original sin," racism, and its continuing effects in our hearts, our churches, and our whole society. We ask you to reflect with us on how racism manifests itself, infecting even our religious communities, and how we as reconciling communities committed to the way of Jesus can confront and transcend this persistent and pervasive evil.

Undoubtedly, all sorts of racism and prejudice pervade American society. We concentrate on black/white racism not simply because it is the most pervasive type and that with which we are most familiar, but because it has engendered some of the richest resources for its eradication through the experience of slavery, its roots in Africa, and the growth of the black church and black theology, all of which continue to transform our understandings of what it means to be Christian. This is not to say that the insights we provide here will not be helpful for addressing other forms of racism and discrimination, such as that which is directed at Hispanics, Asians, Indians, Muslims, gays and lesbians, and other marginalized groups. Yet even as racism has qualities that are common to all its victims, black/white racism has its own special and particularly entrenched nature that deserves particular attention.

We ask you to look with us first at racism and its consequences. Part One offers an examination of conscience for North American Christians. We look first at what racism is and what its contemporary manifestations (chap. 1) are, then at how Christianity itself has been surprisingly yet demonstrably culpable in the development and continuation of racism (chap. 2). We then dive into the silent racism of prejudices and presumptions that informs everyday American life (chap. 3) and the deep myths about body and race and superiority that undergird it (chap. 4). With this base, we ask you to reflect with us on how these patterns play out in America's churches, notably in white Evangelical churches (chap. 5) and the many kinds of black churches (chap. 6). Yet, even as we point to the evil that racism has wrought among us, we also point to signs of hope that inform our larger message.

In Part Two, we turn more deliberately to specific, powerful spiritual and social resources that Christians can cultivate to address racism. We first commend many of the insights of African religion into community, creation, and culture (chap. 7). These lead directly to a spirituality of reconciliation and a practice of restorative love (chap. 8), a contemporary technique that draws directly from the example and preaching of Jesus. Then we invite readers to meditate with us on how our personal, historical, and societal suffering can draw us into a profound sense of our own worth and purpose in life (chap. 9). We show how this profoundly Christian contemplative tradition can be nurtured in our spiritual lives, making room for the Spirit and freeing us to live for and find Christ in our brothers and sisters (chap. 10). Finally, we focus on four practical ways that all Christians—black and white, mainline and evangelical—can promote racial reconciliation in church and community (chap. 11).

Who We Are

We come to this book from decidedly different backgrounds. Michael is an African American who grew up in a middle-class black neighborhood in Raleigh, North Carolina, during which time he was bused an hour each way to attend integrated schools. At age nineteen, he was ordained as a minister of the National Baptist Convention, a historically black church. Through his education at the University of Notre Dame, Duke University, Princeton Theological Seminary (during which time he changed to the Episcopal/ Anglican tradition), and Yale University, he continued to learn to negotiate the biracial worlds of black and white people. From 1993 to 1994 he lived in residence with Archbishop Desmond Tutu in Cape Town, South Africa, where he was ordained as an Anglican priest and studied Tutu's *Ubuntu* theology. These experiences of living well between black and white worlds led to his academic interest in pursuing a theology that articulates God's reconciling work among different cultures and races.

Tony is a white Italian American born and raised in west Philadelphia, a then mostly white neighborhood that now is predominantly black. The Baptist church that he attended there refused to accept black people into its membership, a choice that eventually led to the death of that church. At that point, Tony's father advocated that they follow the basic Baptist principle to ally themselves with the nearest Baptist church, which in this case was an African American church. It is there, at Mount Carmel Baptist church, that Tony has maintained his membership at a black church for the last forty years and is acknowledged as a pastoral associate. In that time, Tony has become one of the best-known and outspoken Evangelicals in America, one who has not been afraid to court controversy, such as taking stances for social justice that often go against the grain of popular evangelicalism and serving as President Clinton's chaplain following the Monica Lewinsky scandal.

Tony and Michael began working together toward the goal of racial reconciliation among Christians in the summer of 1985. Then a college student, Michael traveled to Philadelphia to work with Tony's Evangelical Association for the Promotion of Education (EAPE), where he served for two years, helping to translate the black experience for many white volunteers in the inner city. In addition, Michael traveled with Tony to England and worked with him during his seminary experience, with Tony serving as his Clinical Pastoral Experience (CPE) supervisor. Our conversations on the topic of racial reconciliation continued over the years, and it was in 2001 that we finally decided to move forward on writing this book together. We did so, recognizing that our journeys correlate in different ways, with Michael starting in the black church and moving into the white church, and Tony starting in a white church and moving into a black church. There is also the irony of how our personalities illustrate the "coincidence" of racial reconciliation and defy stereotypes: Tony has often been cited as a white man who has a traditionally "black" preaching style, while Michael is often characterized more by the contemplative traditions associated with white churches.

Grounded in Baptism

We are two men who, at least at first glance, seem to be quite different—white and black, evangelical and Anglican, sociologist and theologian—yet who have discovered their commonality through a common faith in Christ and the conviction that racism, unless it is faced head-on, will continue to wield its deadly force on the church and the country we love. We advocate neither a default mode of Christianity (such as civil religion) nor the belittlement of those who define Christianity differently (such as Pentecostals). What we do claim is that Christian identity is not secondary to racial identity but is in fact our primary identity, in which we are able to negotiate how diverse human cultures may flourish. We believe that our baptism creates a primary identity in Christ, in whom there is no division. Therefore, instead of a stereotypical Christianity that is of no earthly use or, at best, serves as some kind of civil religion used for formal occasions, we believe our primary identity is revealed in Christ, who reconciles the whole world.

We are not naïve, however. We realize the idealism of our claim. This is why our Christian practices become all the more important. Through frank discussions of key historical, social, and ecclesial issues, we seek to test our own convictions and to invite you to do the same. Some of those convictions may at times trouble, provoke, or even offend many readers. Make no mistake: Racism is an offense against the Lord whom we serve and to whom we owe our lives, and must be dealt with as such. Yet we do not wish to present you with a treatise or a shaming harangue, but to engage you with the contemporary enigmas of being Christians with dueling, seemingly conflicting identities, such as black Episcopalian, rich evangelical, white Pentecostal, and so forth. More than that, we seek freedom from what often enslaves well-meaning Christians. In short, this book is an evangelical plea to gird ourselves with the courage to speak the truth in love about God's intention to reconcile all peoples. And as will become evident as you read this book, even as we explore those dueling identities, it is to our Lord that we wish to continually draw your attention, as the One who can heal our disfiguration from racism, and remake us in his image.

Part One

AN ENSLAVED CHURCH

CHAPTER 1

What Is Racism?

Our greatest imperative today is to grasp and confront the reatlity of racism.

A s Christians in North America, we must first acknowledge that racism itself is a continuing and deeply embedded issue in American culture. This truth about the ongoing perniciousness of racism is less evident than it may first appear. After all, since institutional segregation began meeting its demise fifty years ago with the *Brown v. Board of Education* court decision and, most significantly, the Civil Rights Act of 1965, racists in the United States no longer have as many overt ways to practice racism. Old-fashioned racist behaviors, such as "separate but equal" public facilities or race-based job and housing discrimination, are no longer legal, much less considered appropriate or socially accept able. As a result, defining and identifying racism today is difficult because it has gone underground, so to speak. Instead, the ongo-ing effects of America's long history of racism are more likely to be expressed in abstract terms or in covert and subtle ways. What has not changed, however, is that racism is based on the assump-tions that blacks are inferior and whites are superior. Changes in law and practice have done little to change the negative effects that accompany those beliefs. Rather, when racist practices are made illegal or declared unacceptable in the public arena, such effects become submerged, and thus easier to deny or ignore.

Modern Racism

Most of the insidious effects of racism in American society today occur in two ways. The first is when racists in powerful positions are able to have a surreptitiously negative effect on the lives of people of color. This is not to say that all modern racism is practiced by people who consider themselves or their behavior to be deliberately "racist," per se. Indeed, the racist label now carries many shameful connotations that most people are loathe to acknowledge and wish to avoid. Rather, it is the second way racism occurs, which is through people who are trying to "do the right thing" but, out of naïveté or unexplored feelings of racial bias, behave in ways that perpetuate the results of "old-fashioned" racism. Valerie Batts, executive director of Visions Inc., a multiculturalism consultation and training organization defines modern racism according to five dominant behaviors of white people:

> *Most of the insidious effects of racism in American society today occur in two ways. The first is when racists in powerful positions are able to have a surreptitiously negative effect on the lives of people of color.*

1. Dysfunctional rescuing
2. Blaming the victim
3. Avoiding contact
4. Denying differences
5. Denying the political significance of differences[1]

Dysfunctional rescuing takes place when white people take a patronizing or condescending stance toward people of color, most often perceiving blacks as unable to help themselves and thus in need of their assistance. Another dimension of dysfunctional rescuing is behaviors that set people of color up to fail. For instance, efforts to create more racially inclusive workplaces often collapse because those who initiate such efforts, even if their impulses are honorable, fail to prepare the work culture adequately for such changes. Reluctance or hostility toward such inclusivity in the workplace may be denied or overlooked, setting up for potential failure a person of color who has been brought into an environment that lacks a plan for its cultural change. This process of doing what's right without preparing is often called *tokenism*.

Blaming the victim is attributing systemic oppression to the one who suffers under it. For example, if a person of color brought into this hostile environment starts exhibiting paranoid or other inappropriate behaviors, that person's supervisor might recommend psychiatric treatment for his or her emotional shortcomings rather than explore how the workplace culture contributes to those problems.

Avoiding contact takes place when white people segregate themselves in primarily white communities, fail to educate themselves about life in communities of color, and choose not to develop relationships with people of color. In the workplace, such avoidance might manifest itself if, for instance, a supervisor neglects or ignores the interpersonal difficulties between two African American employees in ways he or she would not with white employees.

Denying cultural differences occurs when white people attempt to minimize the obvious physical, cultural, or behavioral differences of people of color, particularly when such factors may play a crucial role in bridging racial divides. For instance, the white supervisor in the scenarios just described may choose to ignore that the workplace has a predominantly "white" culture and that it is having a negative effect on the retention of black employees, or even to recognize that those employees may experience such cultural differences negatively.

Denying the political significance of differences is identified as minimizing the differing influence that social, political, economic, historical, and psychological realities have on the lives of people of color and whites. Some may express the opinion that such cultural differences have only to do with surface appearances and fail to acknowledge how such realities contribute to ongoing racial inequality. In the workplace, this might be expressed through neglect or even negation of affirmative action measures. For instance, in one company, when a supervisor was confronted about the lack of people of color in the workplace, he responded that this had to do with the recent elimination of most entry-level positions, as if those were the only jobs for which a person of color would be suited.

Internalized Racism

Racism in American society doesn't have to do simply with the behaviors and attitudes of white people toward people of color. A significant dimension of racism's embedded character involves internalized racism on the part of people of color. Batts deepens her exploration of modern racism by identifying five internalized oppressions that parallel the five racist behaviors discussed above:

1. Beating the system
2. Blaming the system
3. Avoiding contact
4. Denying of cultural heritage
5. Lack of understanding or minimization of the political significance of racial oppression[2]

Beating the system occurs when people of color try to get around the system by avoiding or failing to develop necessary life skills that are usually deemed necessary for succeeding in most endeavors. In the workplace, this might be recognized in a person of color who manages to advance through company ranks by relying on others who can cover for his or her failure to develop adequate tools such as verbal or writing skills to accomplish job requirements.

Blaming the system occurs when persons of color assign responsibility for their failures onto the structures that were supposed to prepare them to succeed but do not consider their personal roles in such failures. For instance, if the inadequately skilled employee in the above example is fired or demoted, he or she may blame the company for its failure to provide adequate training rather than consider his or her lack of personal preparation.

Avoiding contact here is the internalized oppression converse of the racist behavior and is displayed when people of color try to avoid contact with whites or take a stance of distrusting all whites, isolating themselves in communities of color even when an advantageous opportunity to move into a racially mixed community presents itself. But this dimension has a deeper aspect, in that people of color may also reject other people of color whom they perceive as not being "black enough," perhaps because of a

> *Some persons of color deliberately shed their cultural distinctiveness out of a belief in the superiority or comparative advantages of white culture.*

lighter skin tone or because of cultural preferences that seem to mirror white culture. It is not unusual to hear an African American refer to another black person as an "Uncle Tom" when that person has successfully negotiated a prominent position in a predominantly white workplace.

Denying cultural heritage happens when persons of color show preference for whites out of a distrust of their own group. In the workplace, a person of color may attempt to ingratiate him- or herself with white supervisors and avoid black supervisors out of a perception that the latter are less skilled or less well regarded in the organization. It may also be recognized in persons of color who deliberately shed their cultural distinctiveness out of a belief in the superiority or comparative advantages of white culture.

Lack of understanding or minimization of the political significance of racial oppression differs from its counterpart in the five dimensions of modern racism in that it is manifest in passive and unassertive behaviors on the part of persons of color. It also demonstrates itself in persons of color who discriminate against other persons of color whom they perceive to be less powerful, usually as an expression of their own feelings of powerlessness. In the workplace, a black supervisor may be harder on other persons of color whom they supervise or show inappropriate deference to white persons with more power.

A Politics of Resignation

These dynamics of modern racism can be recognized not only on interpersonal levels, such as workplaces or educational settings, but also in larger structural and organizational levels. Melvin Peters, a professor of religion at Duke University, has spoken of a "politics of resignation," which seems not only to capture several of these dimensions of modern and internalized racism, but also to describe the obsession and need of both blacks and whites to categorize people into racial affinity organizations, whether those be positive forces for social change, such as the NAACP (National Association for the Advancement of Colored Persons), or white supremacy groups such as the KKK (Ku Klux Klan). Peters writes:

> The proliferation of such organizations and the on-going comfort level that we all seem to feel about their presence in our society indicate that, for the most of us, there is nothing unusual about the fundamental premise upon which they rest. The premise seems to be this: the physical differences between people are firm, necessary, significant, insurmountable, constant, valuable, unchanging, and for some, divinely ordered. Or to paraphrase the lines of a poem I learned some time ago, "Oh Black is black and white is white and never the twain shall meet."[3]

Accepting this principle, most of us no longer debate the obvious fallacies that underlie modern racism. Instead, we adopt coping strategies that facilitate our continued existence as discrete, impenetrable subcultures within a human population out of a conviction that we are never going to change existing conditions in our lifetime.

This assumption of immutability—this politics of resignation—reinforces the activity not only of specialized groups, but of whole institutions in our society—political parties, churches, universities, foundations, and the like. Thus, we are more likely to hear and accept talk of the black vote, the Jewish lobby, minority fellowships, white school districts, the Hispanic community, black theology, and the like. Few question the origins of the categories that divide us; most simply accept them as there. In our behavior we seem to echo the lines of a popular hymn:

The rich man in his castle, the poor man at his gate,
God made them high or lowly and ordered their estate.
All things bright and beautiful, all creatures great and small,
All things wise and wonderful the Lord God made them all.[4]

Our comfort with the status quo—our politics of resignation—has clear advantages for both whites and persons of color and has served both well in many instances. By seeking out, relating to, and defending the interests of our peer group, we find emotional peace, affirmation, and a sense of well-being. This might be unproblematic if all groups were afforded opportunities to defend their interests in relative peace, and if those interests were not in conflict. But the unpleasant truth of our time is this: We are threatening to destroy not only each other but also the fragile planet on which we live by our continued and dogged pursuit of individual and subgroup self-interests.

> *The unpleasant truth of our time is this: We are threatening to destroy, not only each other, but also the fragile planet on which we live by our continued and dogged pursuit of individual/group self-interests.*

This persistence should trouble us all and prompt us to explore an alternative process that counters the prevailing politics of resignation. We call this counter-process a "politics of education" (of self and of other) with respect to human difference. The recovery of one's own cultural roots is vital to the dignity of any peoples who have recently been, or still are, oppressed by people of other cultures. As we explore the reality of racism in Christian churches and set forth a vision of reconciliation that is grounded in a broad-based Christian understanding, the politics of education will form the foundation of our proposals. But first we must understand how the politics of resignation has taken root in both white and black Christian churches and exacerbated the imbeddedness of racism in American culture.

CHAPTER 2

Christianity and Racism

Christianity has been deeply compromised by its participation in a culture of racism.

There is no longer Jew *or* Greek, there is no longer slave *or* free, there is no longer *male* and *female*; for all of you are one in Christ Jesus. (Galatians 3:28; emphasis ours)

This biblical passage, attributed to the apostle Paul, has long been the ground from which those seeking racial reconciliation, including ourselves, have made the case for a church that believes and acts on the notion that being free in Christ means that there are no racial divisions in our Christian baptism. Unfortunately, many in the Western church read this verse to mean that human unity is found in some kind of conglomerate of heterogeneous persons bound together primarily by individualistic spirituality. In that view, there really is no unity in Christ, only convenient alliances between Christians. Such alliances, however, have grave consequences, and not just because they aid and abet the kinds of modern and internalized racism we discussed in chapter 1. For example, consider this passage from *The Autobiography of Malcolm X*, where he criticizes Christian complicity in a racist culture. He asks black Christians to examine their own images of God to ascertain whether even they might be infected:

Brothers and sisters, the white man has brainwashed us black people to fasten our gaze upon a blond-haired, blue-eyed Jesus!

11

We're worshiping a Jesus that doesn't even look like us! Now, just think of this. The blond-haired, blue-eyed white man has taught you and me to worship a white Jesus, and to shout and sing and pray to this God that's his God, the white man's God. The white man has taught us to shout and sing and pray until we die, to wait until death, for some dreamy heaven-in-the-hereafter, when we're dead, while this white man has his milk and honey in the streets paved with golden dollars right here on this earth![1]

The profound question that Malcolm X raises for Christians is, To what degree has the Christian church formed an alliance with one dominant racial and cultural perspective to which all other human diversity is to conform? In other words, *Is the church enslaved by the white, European perspective?* To get at an answer to this key question, we must look at racial divisions in the Christian church from a historical point of view.

Racial Divisions in Historical Perspective

Martin Luther King Jr.'s statement that 10:00 AM on Sunday morning is the most segregated hour in North America has haunted the Christian church for over forty years, but the practices that prompted those words had been in place for centuries before they were ever uttered. Given the brutality of the so-called peculiar institution of slavery in America, one naturally wonders why so many African Americans emerged from slavery as self-declared Christians. After all, it is not as if whites Christianized black slaves without misgivings or in order to incorporate them into their congregations as full and equal members. Indeed, some clergy reprimanded slaveholders for neglecting the salvation of their servants and evangelized slaves themselves when possible. However, no institutional attempt to confront the task of slave conversion in English colonial America was made until the Society for the Propagation of the Gospel in Foreign Parts became active (Founded in London in 1701 as a missionary arm of the Church of England, the society ministered to the colonists of America and also instructed the Native Americans and blacks) there. Its conversion methods stressed religious instruction.[2] Moreover, as we note below, slave conversion was neither immediate nor without perplexing difficulties for the white evangelists.

Neither the halting efforts to evangelize slaves nor the slaveholders' reluctance to worship with them as equals resulted in the rapid creation of black churches. Indeed, the white overlords were afraid of allowing black people to have their own churches. They were conscious that if leaders emerged within black churches they could encourage an African American movement that would threaten white hegemony in the South's political economic system. Consequently, they kept black slaves within their own confines, requiring them to worship with their white masters but making them sit in the church balconies while the main floors were reserved for the white congregants.

> Given the brutality of the so-called peculiar institution of slavery in America, one naturally wonders why so many African Americans emerged from slavery as self-declared Christians.

Within this tension between conversion and control, we begin to see the problem of an enslaved church, one in which the powerful whites made their African slaves choose between Jesus's baptism and the white man's version of Christianity. As African slaves slowly began to break from their masters on religious matters and black Christian thinkers began to question slaveholding religion, making the right choice thus became a common theme for black Christians worldwide.

Understanding the early history of the relationship between slaveholding and Christianity in America helps us get at the problem of the "convenient alliances" that have resulted from our misreading of Galatians 3:28. Abolitionist Frederick Douglass wrote forcefully on this issue. He was particularly troubled by how freed slaves of African descent could believe in the religion of their white masters who prayed with blacks on Sunday but beat them on Monday. This led him to make a distinction between "slaveholding religion" and Christianity proper. That is, he could only reconcile the true Christian church—represented by Jesus's baptism—by naming its false twin "slaveholding religion," a term that is still in use today. For Douglass, God moved within U. S. history to carry the slaves to freedom, just as he did in Egypt at the time of Moses and the Hebrew slaves. (One might say that Douglass embraced liberation theology before it rose to prominence in the last half of the twentieth century.) White Christians often used their version of Christianity, slaveholding religion, to legitimate the oppressive social structures that kept blacks "in their place."

White Christians often used their version of Christianity ("slaveholding religion") to legitimate the oppressive social structures that kept blacks "in their place."

By the early nineteenth century, white control over black worship began to break down in the South as well as the North. Indeed, there is some evidence that the South was as critical of slavery as the North. For instance, North Carolina formed a state antislavery society in 1816 and by 1826 led all states with forty-five such societies. Blacks began forming their own churches, most notably the African Methodist Episcopal Church (A.M.E.), which was founded in 1816 by former slave Richard Allen when he broke off from white Methodists. Similarly, what would later be called the National Baptist Convention was formed in 1880 following a protest against years of blacks not being welcomed among white Baptists.

But in the 1830s, where slavery and emancipation were concerned, church leaders in all major white communions (except the Society of Friends) were at best only moderates. Although they may have disagreed with slavery they hesitated to engage in any concerted action to end it. Sympathies were clearly with colonialists (sympathies for stable government, the protection of majority rights, and the need for workforce), not with immediate emancipationists. Scripture is ambiguous at best regarding slavery, and a distinct sanction for the social condition of black people is stated in Genesis 9:25: "Cursed be Canaan; a slave of slaves shall he be to his brothers." Interpreting slavery as the basis for racial division within the church continued to justify white people as the chosen people of God, and thus legitimated the peculiar duty given to white people to control black people under the Christian economy. To call slavery "sinful" was, in effect, to reject the Bible in favor of some rationalistic mode of thought. "Opposition to slavery has never been the offspring of the Bible," said prominent American theologians James Henley Thornwell and Robert Lewis Dabney.

Despite growing opposition to slavery in the South many southern Christian moralists focused on the issue of slavery to the point of charging infidelity of persons or groups who did not agree with the South's position. The debate over slavery caused many white denominations—including Methodists, Baptists, Presbyterians, and Lutherans—to go through structural division. (Episcopalians did not technically split over slavery since the South missed the Episcopal Church's General Conventions beginning in 1861 and slowly began to return in 1865 after the end of the Civil War.) Roman Catholics survived schism by never allowing the slavery question to enter hierarchical discussion. It was not until 1946 that the National Council of Churches condemned segregation as a lack of Christian witness.

Understanding the Black Church Today

Understanding the black church through the "convenient alliance" model is helpful as one looks at it in historical perspective, but in its contemporary context—after the collapse of overt racist behavior in the United States—this model seems less accurate. That is, without a common enemy like racism, the black church seems unintelligible to some observers today. It is necessary, therefore, to find other rubrics under which one can understand the development of the black church in the United States. Michael suggests that the black church can best be understood under white Protestant theologian H. Richard Niebuhr's typology from his book *Christ and Culture*.[3] In this landmark of Christian theology, Niebuhr identified five modes of interaction between his title subjects: 1) Christ against culture, 2) Christ of culture, 3) Christ above culture, 4) Christ transforming culture, and 5) Christ and culture in paradox. The black church sees itself falling in the "Christ against culture" category because of slavery. This means that, for the most part, those who consider themselves part of the black church identify themselves as such because of their shared oppressive history of slavery and its antagonistic relationship with Christianity.

Sociologically, identity is established in a "we/them" opposition. In this case, the black church community braces itself to withstand the onslaught of many enemies, particularly the form of Christianity presented by the white master. As a result, spiritual traditions such as contemplative prayer, spiritual direction, and evangelism to all the world are seldom practiced in the black church because of its need to achieve a specifically "black" identity in opposition to the white churches that have used their past hegemonic privilege to define the dominant church in the United States. Instead, black churches primarily practice a cathartic spirituality that can address issues of particular importance to the black community, such as slavery reparations, racism, drugs, poverty, and corrupt police officers. In order to maintain itself, then, the black church must try to find a new common enemy to take the place of the overt racism that marked America until the last third of the twentieth century.

> *Despite the current ambiguity of the social and political role of the church, its spiritual practices still allow for a sense of human restlessness that instinctively rebels against all forms of oppression and repression.*

While there are other ways to understand the black church phenomenon, most observers basically agree that it is in a crisis of identity. This is true not only of the black church in the United States but also of many African churches formed in other former European colonies. They continue to struggle to establish their identity beyond race. According to South African theologian Charles Villa-Vicencio:

> The institutional churches in many parts of Africa . . . also showed the promise of new life on the eve of independence. Before long, however, they too tumbled into the comfort of their own brand of Constantinian captivity. Churches of the Third World, unable to escape the missionary mode of existence, often reflect values in newly emerged nations in their quest to throw off the last vestiges of the colonial past. Indeed, the role of the different churches in Third World revolutionary and post-revolutionary situations like Nicaragua, the Philippines, Angola, Mozambique and Zimbabwe is politically ambiguous, requiring serious theological review.[4]

Villa-Vicencio reports that not only has the church in the United States fallen into racial division, but racial reconciliation in the church worldwide is lethargic given the social changes that have taken place. In order to envision healing this paralysis, we need to diagnose the root of how this has happened—namely, European colonialism.

But first, we will counter the prevalent sentiment that the church has been irreparably damaged, and is therefore unable to facilitate racial reconciliation. This attitude is an ecclesiastical form of the politics of resignation. We wish to persuade readers that despite the current ambiguity of the social and political role of the church, its spiritual practices still allow for a sense of human restlessness that instinctively rebels against all forms of oppression and repression. Roman Catholic theologian Johan Baptist Metz refers to this kind of spirituality as the "dangerous memory" of the gospel that cannot be ignored. For Metz, one needs the prophetic imagination capable of maintaining the "dangerous memory" of justice in the midst of socialization processes that try to make us forget social justice. A dangerous memory is a theological "given" that ultimately makes the church an uneasy accomplice in any social or political alliance that does not function in the interests of "least of these."[5] In order better to practice this "dangerous memory" of being the church, we will consider the origins of racial divisions and the church's role in facilitating these divisions.

Ecclesial Origins of Racial Divisions

It was the "African" side of black religion that helped African-Americans to see beyond the white distortions of the Gospel and to discover its true meaning as God's liberation of the oppressed from bondage. It was the "Christian" element in black religion that helped African-Americans to re-orient their African past so that it would become useful in the struggle to survive with dignity in a society that they did not make.[6]

These words by the architect of black theology, James Cone, help us to see the great dilemma of the Christian church. On one hand, the church preaches salvation and the liberation of people, and on the other hand, it is complicit in ongoing racial division. We have already briefly discussed the difficult history of Christianity and slavery, but more needs to be said about how the contradiction between Christianity and slavery produced persistent flaws in the early Western churches.

Countering the effects of race as a primary category of human identity will require some effort, but African American sociologist W. E. B. DuBois can help us begin. His classic *The Souls of Black Folk* has influenced many who have sought to develop a more nuanced understanding of racial identity:

It is a peculiar sensation, this double-consciousness, this sense of always looking at one's self through the eyes of others, of measuring one's soul by the tape of a world that looks on in amused contempt and pity. One ever feels his twoness, an American, a Negro; two souls, two thoughts, two unreconciled strivings; two warring ideals in one dark body, whose dogged strength alone keeps it from being torn asunder.[7]

Cone has noted how these "two warring ideals" have marked the North American church from its beginnings up to now, including the debates about "integration" and "inculturation."

Louis Farrakhan, founder of the Nation of Islam, got at one of the problems of black Christian identity when he declared that the white Christian church had offered blacks a blond-haired, blue-eyed Jesus to worship, and he realized that Jesus was neither. By identifying this idolatrous Jesus, Farrakhan drew attention to the fact that the churches of America had given to the black community a Jesus who incarnated white identity and values. When such a Jesus is worshiped, according to Farrakhan, black people end up worshiping everything that the white culture is about. This means that black people end up deifying their oppressors and becoming alienated from their own identity as African Americans.

George Bernard Shaw once said that, "God created us in his image, and we decided to return the favor." What Shaw made clear is similar to what the French sociologist and philosopher Emile Durkheim expounded in his book *The Elementary Forms of the Religious Life.*[8] Trying to understand the origins of religion, Durkheim analyzed a group of aboriginal people who lived in the interior of Australia. He took note of how these aboriginal people developed their concept of God.

In the first stage, a group develops traits and values that make it quite distinct from other groups of people. Sociologists and anthropologists are well aware that members of every group interact in time and space, creating cultural characteristics that are specifically unique. Certainly, African American people know this, and are able to distinguish the traits and values of their own groups from those of the dominant white culture.

The group comes up with an animal to symbolize its traits and values in the second stage of religious development. For example, one group might emphasize the necessity of physical strength among males by making an ox the totem for its tribe (in other words, strong as an ox). A tribe that takes pride in its wisdom might choose the owl to be its totem (that is, wise as an owl). Still another tribe might reflect on its primary asset—the speed at which its people can run—by making the deer its totem (meaning, swift as a deer). The animal totem of the tribe comes to be the embodiment of what the tribe sees as its best qualities.

The third stage is the beginning of the tribe's totem worship. Little by little the totem then becomes the god of the tribe. It is easy to see why Durkheim believed that religion becomes nothing more than a group worshiping itself. After all, if a group ends up worshiping a symbolic representation of its own traits and values, Durkheim's conclusions are obvious—that we end up only worshiping ourselves. Paul states the same notion briefly and distinctly in the Romans 1:19-23:

> For what can be known about God is plain to them, because God has shown it to them. Ever since the creation of the world his eternal power and divine nature, invisible though they are, have been understood and seen through the things he has made. So they are without excuse; for though they knew God, they did not honor him as God or give thanks to him, but they became futile in their thinking, and their senseless minds were darkened. Claiming to be wise, they became fools; and they exchanged the glory of the immortal God for images resembling a mortal human being or birds or four-footed animals or reptiles.

Farrakhan, without taking note of Paul's or Durkheim's writing, was also aware of this phenomenon. He sensed that Christianity had a strong propensity for turning black people into worshipers of a Jesus who incarnates the oppressive white culture and hence compounds African American subservience to it.

If black people are to be free from exploitation by whites, it is important that they have a God who is a liberator rather than an incarnation of their oppressors.

It is obvious that we need to deconstruct Jesus as defined by the white society. If black people are to be free from exploitation by whites, it is important that they have a God who is a liberator rather than an incarnation of their oppressors. To worship the cultural deity that has emerged out of white Christianity is idolatry. And it is this sort of idolatry that Paul condemns in his letter to the Romans.

Tony recalls a time when he walked into his Sunday school class to teach a group of young African American men something about the gospel. When he entered the classroom he immediately noticed that the picture of Jesus (the very famous "Head of Christ" by Warner Sallman) had been removed, and in its place someone had posted a picture of a black Jesus. "Who put that there?" Tony asked with a certain degree of indignation.

"I did," said an angry black teenager.

"Jesus wasn't a black man," Tony snapped back.

"And he wasn't a white man, either," responded the teenager.

The answer to a white Jesus is not to create a black Jesus to take his place. Ethnic groups of any kind need to be delivered from the tendency to worship their own identities. If we all come into relationships with the God who transcends all cultural deities and wants "no graven images," we will take a step toward transcending racism. Quakers and Mennonites have long understood that all portrayals of Jesus end up as idolized images of people's perceptions of themselves. Their houses of worship historically were devoid of any paintings of Christ because they knew that the Christian God transcends the gods of the culture.

Unfortunately, in this day of a multitude of Christian denominations, few seem able or willing to confess that the church has been complicit in the sin of racism by promoting a white Jesus, thus allowing Christian identity to become secondary to these oppressive racial identities. Few confess that the church played an ambiguous role in *constructing* these racial identities, especially in African societies throughout the colonial period. Missionaries actively promoted colonial advances into African communities, and in some instances even welcomed military aggression against particular tribes in Africa on the basis that they were "more heathen" than other African peoples. This created another level of injustice within the church because the sacrifice and service of these African peoples took place for the benefit of many other Africans who became Christians. For example, South African president Nelson Mandela has stated that he would not have become who he is without Christian missionaries. And yet, the defeat of African chiefs, the shattered morale of the people, the loss of land, the confiscation of cattle, and the collapse of African cultures created an environment within which missionary attempts to lure Africans into their missions became that much easier. Because of this ambiguity, for many Africans there was no salvation outside of the European church since it was often an institution within the oppressive colonial empires that decided who should die or live according to racial identity.

Initially, the majority of African chiefs rejected Christian missions. Missionary endeavors met with a measure of success only when the socioeconomic, political, and cultural structures of diverse African societies began to crumble in the wake of the frontier wars in which Europeans began to take over African lands. These successes can also be partly attributed to the differing cosmologies of the African and European peoples. The African cosmology did not regard God's creation as something to own or even control, while the European Christian cosmology was yoked with European cultural sensibilities of land ownership and colonialism. As a result, the land contracts that Europeans proffered were counterintuitive to African sensibilities, and Africans were thus left at a disadvantage. Compounding the cosmological differences between European and African peoples was the almost universal lack, in sub-Saharan African cultures, of the sorts literary materials by which Europeans measured intelligence.

In light of this cosmological and intellectual conflict between Africa and Europe, it is not difficult to imagine European exegesis of Jesus's Great Commission, Matthew 28:18-20:

> All authority in heaven and on earth has been given to me. Go therefore and make disciples of all nations, baptizing them in the name of the Father and of the Son and of the Holy Spirit, and teaching them to obey everything that I have commanded you. And remember, I am with you always, to the end of the age.

Many European Christians interpreted becoming a Christian under the Great Commission as being the same as becoming Westernized: living in square houses, wearing Western-style clothes, and participating in the colonial economy. Further, many European missionaries even thought that Africans were especially deprived and required another kind of salvation, different from Europeans, who were closer to God.

In America, this European understanding of the special deprivation of Africans is illustrated through the slave evangelism efforts the Reverend Francis Le Jau, an Anglican priest stationed at the Goose Creek parish near Charleston, South Carolina. Reverend Le Jau reported the extreme difficulties of Native American and African conversion ministry in an outpost of the British empire. He believed that Africans in this British outpost required even more supernatural intervention in order for them to be saved. A few slaves did become Christians, often against the wishes of planters who feared that baptism would lead to social revolution. African slaves had to consent to the following declaration:

> You declare in the Presence of God and before this Congregation that you do not ask for the holy baptism out of any design to free yourself from the Duty and Obedience you owe to your Master while you live, but merely for the good of your Soul and to partake of the Graces and Blessings promised to the Members of the Church of Jesus Christ.[9]

In short, Christian missions were successful in Africa because Christianity arrived accompanied by the military and commercial might of the Western nations. They were especially successful in the nineteenth and twentieth centuries among peoples who had, until that time, practiced African traditional religions. The battle cry for early Christian missionaries from Britain and Europe was to burn the fetishes of the heathen. Later, we will explore more closely the differences between North American black theology and African theology. For now, it suffices to say that while the black church has been grounded in a theology of liberation, its main thrust is still to adapt to the Western world.

A Critique from Black Theology

If we are to learn how the enslaved church may be free, it would be wise not to repeat the same mistakes of our past. One way not to repeat such mistakes is to listen to the prophetic voices that warn us of our sins, such as that of James Cone. The crucial idea we are to learn from Cone, one that embarrasses the church, is that *African* and *Christian* are contradictory terms for most people. Cone believes that black religious thought is neither identical with white American Christian theology nor identical with traditional African beliefs. Instead, says Cone, it is the black people's struggle for justice in a nation dominated by white racist structures that is the primary context of black religious life.

> *Recovering their own cultural roots is vital to the dignity of any peoples who have recently been, or still are, oppressed by people of other cultures.*

Cone's critique teaches us that the African element continued to play an important role in defining the core of black religion, thus preventing it from becoming merely an imitation of Protestant or Catholic theologies in the West. Of course, for Cone, black religious thought and white Protestant and Catholic reflections on the Christian tradition are quite similar, but he stresses that:

the *dissimilarities* between them are perhaps more important than the similarities. The similarities are found at the point of common Christian identity, and the dissimilarities can best be understood in light of the differences between African and European cultures in the New World. While whites used their cultural perspective to dominate others, blacks used theirs to affirm their dignity and to empower themselves to struggle for justice. The major reason for the differences between black and white reflections on God is found at the point of the great differences in life. As white theology is largely defined by its response to modern and post-modern societies of Europe and America, usually ignoring the contradictions of slavery and oppression in black life; black religious thought is the thinking of slaves and of marginalized blacks whose understanding of God was shaped by the very contradictions that white theologians ignored and regarded as unworthy of serious theological reflection.[10]

Yet, while adapting Christianity is always possible because of the relevance of the gospel to any culture, particularizing it can be misunderstood to threaten the universal relevance of the gospel to all cultures. Recovering their own cultural roots is vital to the dignity of any peoples who have recently been, or still are, oppressed by people of other cultures. Especially on account of the tension between the universality and particularity inherent in the Christian vision, it is, however always a pity when this leads to the narrowing perspective of a hegemonic Christ, such as the one white masters offered to their slaves or the one European missionaries preached in Africa, or any under which the church in America still struggles. In the next chapter we will explore further how the legacies of racism and an enslaved church have an ongoing effect on church and culture.

CHAPTER 3

Ongoing Legacies of Racism

Let's be honest with each other—and with ourselves—about everyday racism.

Although we could point to numerous legacies of racism in both church and society, one of its key features that is too often overlooked but deserves closer scrutiny here is the culture of dishonesty that has arisen around race. As noted in chapter 1, overt racism has, in the past half-century, given way to more subtle forms of modern and internalized racism; the more open expressions that marked so much of American society from its formation are now mostly treated as shameful and unacceptable. Likewise, in the church, virtually every major Protestant denomination in the United States has developed antiracism initiatives and encouraged their congregations to open themselves to greater racial diversity. Yet the separation of white church and black church remains entrenched. Denominational initiatives often come across as mere lip service with little commitment. Moreover, even though most Christians quickly acknowledge racism as sinful, when one attempts to discuss issues of racism in many, if not most, white churches, it too often is treated with discomfort or dismissiveness: "We don't have any black people in our neighborhood so it's not an issue for us"; "It's no big deal—we welcome anyone who shows up"; or "African Americans have honorable church traditions that serve them just fine; why should we make a special effort to diversify?" While progress in racial equality in church and society is not to be treated with disregard, the shame and sense of sinfulness that is now attached to racism has, in many cases, made it more difficult to discuss the topic openly and honestly, particularly in racially mixed situations.

Strengthening Black Families

Some of the silence about racism may have its roots in studies of African American life at the height of the Civil Rights era and their recommendations for a policy of "benign neglect" toward the problems they uncovered. During the 1960s, the late New York senator Daniel P. Moynihan, while serving as a special adviser to President Richard M. Nixon, submitted a report to the administration that had social scientists and the public talking and reflecting upon its contents for years to come.[1] What Moynihan said, in essence, was that great social problems existed in the black community, due primarily to its weak family system. He went on to point out that in the days of slavery, family solidarity was discouraged primarily because strong family ties would make it difficult to punish disobedient slaves without getting a reaction from other family members. Worse, when slaves had to be sold off or separated from their immediate families, there could be significant trouble among the blacks. Hence, according to Moynihan, slave owners made sure that they encouraged weak family relationships.

One legacy produced by this pattern of weak family relationships is the longstanding and all-too-common sexual exploitation of black women, particularly in the South. If strong family ties were more prevalent in the African American community, such exploitation would likely be more strongly resisted. Instead, Moynihan argued, racist power systems have established a familial model that promotes patterns of irresponsible African American male behavior, which has created a pathological culture passed on from generation to generation up to the present. Moynihan concluded that the sociocultural problems in the black community today are the result of developments occurring over a long period of time and that government-sponsored social programs cannot correct immediately. To the consternation of many progressive thinkers, the report suggested that the government might be wise to exercise what Moynihan called " benign neglect." This made it seem that, unless the black community could get its act together and facilitate stable family life over a period of decades, there was little hope for improving their lot in American society.

Moynihan's thesis elicited an intense negative response. The report ignored the reality that family stability is closely related to economic opportunities. Both then and now, the concept of the man being "the good provider" has shaped American social attitudes. When a man cannot get a job and adequately support his family, he is much more likely to disengage from or leave it. Studies indicate a strong correspondence between black men finding gainful employment and their being an active part of a strong family. That African American families often seem to be matrifocal is not due to cultural tendencies inherent in the African American community but rather because American society has always had better job opportunities for black women than for black men. Even in

> *We do not deny that the African American community has a weak family system. But we believe the answer does not lie in benign neglect but in the government ensuring that there are jobs.*

the days of the postbellum South, when men could not find employment women could almost always take in laundry, help white families raise children, do cooking and cleaning, and carry out a host of other domestic tasks. Those who exercise the most economic power in the household also possess the most political power, and, historically, household decision making is weighted in favor of the primary wage earner. Under the continuing American bias toward male family dominance, therefore, when a man finds himself unemployable, he loses domestic power almost completely and thus is more likely to withdraw from his family in humiliation. Sociologist Elliot Liebow's famous study, *Talley's Corner*, in its examination of young men who hang out on street corners, dramatically showed how a lack of jobs results in family irresponsibility.[2]

We do not deny that the African American community has a weak family system. But we believe the solution does not lie in benign neglect, as Moynihan suggested, but rather in the government ensuring that there are jobs. More recently, sociologist William Julius Wilson, in his book *The Truly Disadvantaged*, showed that many African American women are not interested in getting married simply because they believe that black men are financial burdens and that marrying them will mean supporting them economically. This explains why Wilson found that many black women in poor communities wanted to have children but did not want to get married. Their maternal instincts were as strong as ever but the thought of having a legal relationship (marriage) with an unemployed male was undesirable.[3]

In another book, *When Work Disappears*, Wilson pointed out that a lack of jobs tends to create all the negative social characteristics in any soociety that whites often believe are endemic to African American culture. To make his case, he cited a village in Switzerland whose economy was built around watch making. When the wind-up watches for which Switzerland was famous passed out of style, this village's people lost their primary means of economic support. The government came in and provided monies through an extensive welfare system for the families' survival. Yet, within just a few years, village life collapsed, and these previously productive Swiss began exhibiting laziness, sexual irresponsibility, and the total disintegration of family life. Through such a case we can see that the same characteristics that have marked negative images of black culture among white people are a direct result of economic circumstances and have nothing to do with biological factors or ethnic inheritance.[4]

When African Americans Are Absent

There is more, of course, to the problem of silence around racism issues than simply an ongoing practice of benign neglect. In one of our conversations together as we planned this book, we happened upon the uneasy question, What happens among white people when black people are absent or not around? Is there more freedom to express more authentic thoughts about black people in their absence? We knew the other side of the spectrum, through the creative mind of Ralph Ellison in his classic novel *Invisible Man*, what black people say when white people are not around.[5] Unlike Ellison, however, we are focusing on black absence to get at the cause of an enslaved church, the problem of disproportionate power in a church that allegedly follows one who gave up power, Jesus Christ. To examine this ongoing problem of power (as opposed to prejudice) in racism we need to address with insight and honesty these questions: What do white Christians say when black people are not around? Do white Christians lack honesty and truth-telling when it comes to race relations?

We assert that a different kind of conversation does indeed go on among white people when African Americans are not present. They often express viewpoints that they honestly hold and that they would be embarrassed to express if African Americans were in the same room. The stereotypes and negative images that have characterized the dominant white society conversation readily surface. Whites more readily express their common belief that African Americans have a distinctive culture that they deem inferior to the dominant white culture. As African Americans have asserted themselves by claiming a distinct ethnic identity, their white neighbors have readily acceded to that claim. But, in private, those same white neighbors often exhibit an ethnocentric disposition that assigns inferiority to those who have been acculturated into an African American mind-set.

Prominent spokespersons within the African American community are now beginning to voice these thoughts that white people are afraid to articulate when black people are around. Consider the writings of Shelby Steele, an African American social scientist from San Jose State University. In his book *The Content of Our Character*, Steele argues that over the past fifty years—that is, the last two generations—the larger African American community has often purposely chosen to identify itself in terms of behavioral patterns that represent some of the worst traits evidenced in the African American underclass. Steele argues that African American young people increasingly identify with patterns of behavior that encourage sexual promiscuity, an absence of socially accepted manners and dress styles, and a denigration of academic pursuits.[6]

Analogously, several years ago the late sociologist Stanford Lyman delivered a series of lectures on racism in which he pointed out that during the days of slavery African Americans often feigned laziness and ignorance as a survival technique in order to lower the expectations of their slave owners. By pretending to be lazy and unable to understand what was being asked of them, they could avoid additional work that made their daily load too much to bear. The slaves found that they would not be severely punished when they took these sorts of necessary risks to get relief from their arduous labors, and thus this survival technique worked very well for them.

> *The African American community has often purposely chosen to identify itself in terms of behavioral patterns that represent some of the worst traits evidenced in the African American underclass.*

The popular 1970s TV series *Roots* brilliantly displayed this "con job" that blacks played on their white masters. *Roots* showed that when black people were by themselves they talked and behaved one way but when they were in front of their white masters they conned them by pretending to be less intelligent and hardworking than they really were. Lyman asked the black students he had assembled, "At what point did the con job that the slaves played on their masters become an image that they themselves believed? In other words, in conning the masters did they not also con themselves? Could it be that the image that they projected for survival became the image that they themselves tended to believe?" These questions, which neither Lyman nor his hearers attempted to answer, left his audience in stunned silence and deep reflection.

These self-defeating behaviors may evidence an inferiority complex among many in the African American community that is an ongoing legacy of racism; that is, the deemed "inferiority" of

African American culture that characterizes white viewpoints may be having a shaping effect on the black community.

Tony recalls a conversation he had with two African American government officials regarding social policies that affect the education of young African Americans. He posed the question to them, "Do you gentlemen really believe that African American young people are capable of learning at the same level as whites? Let's cut all the politically correct ways of speaking; tell me the truth. Do you really think that if the same kind of learning opportunities were available for blacks as there are for whites that black young people would do as well as their white counterparts?" After an embarrassed pause, both officials admitted that no matter what is done in the near future, black young people will not be able to learn at a level that meets societal expectations or will enable them to keep up with white young people. They went on to point out that they did not believe that this was because black people are intellectually inferior but that the socialization of African American children—most of whom are perceived as living below the poverty level—predisposes them to academic failure. They pointed out that black children in urban America watch television much more than white children do; one official cited a study of youngsters in the city of Baltimore, where African American young people watch television more than five hours a day, on average. The homes of these children have few, if any, books available, and reading is a rare pastime. The other official cited statistics from the heavily African American city of Camden, New Jersey, where 92 percent of the births in one year were children born out of wedlock. He said, "Children growing up in poor single-family homes just do not have the kind of support that they need to succeed in school."

The Evangelical Association for the Promotion of Education (EAPE), which Tony heads up, has established summer programs for children and teenagers who live in housing projects in nine cities across North America. The ministry staff workers report an ongoing problem for African American young people who want to do well and who are encouraged to do well in school. When these young people—high school students in particular—take learning seriously they are often "ruffed up" by their African American peers who accuse them of "acting white" because they carry books home from school in order to do their homework. One youngster who had an affinity for classical music was surrounded by a group of tough fellow students from his school who took away his violin and busted it to pieces as they accused him of selling out to the white establishment. This leads us both to ask the question, When did learning become a white thing?

African American Self-Critique

Another story Tony tells is of a meeting he was part of several years ago—the kind of story that is readily related when black people are not around. The meeting was held under the auspices of the city tenant council of a new government housing project in Philadelphia. In this particular housing project, the EAPE had recruited a group of thirty young people—almost exclusively white university students—who established summer programs in the project, including recreation, cultural enrichment, and Bible study. These university students had volunteered to work without pay through the entire summer and even traveled to Philadelphia at their own expense. They did the work that paid social workers and recreational workers hired by the city were supposed to be doing. The professional workers were seldom seen in the government housing project, basically reneging on their responsibilities.

As the EAPE workers gained significant recognition within the project, a story appeared in the Philadelphia newspaper describing their accomplishments. The African American paid professionals were embarrassed by the article, which reported that the EAPE volunteers were doing all the work that the city had hired the professionals to do. They reacted by getting the tenant council, made up of elected members of the community, to call a meeting with the expressed purpose of voting to oust the EAPE programs.

At the meeting, which Tony attended, the paid professionals had made sure to stack the proceedings in their favor: the room was filled with neighborhood residents. The professionals said that they wanted to shut down the EAPE programs because the university student volunteers were "imposing white middle-class values on the neighborhood children." They continued their argument, using the all-too-common rhetoric heard from too many such professionals, stating how the values communicated by these EAPE workers made the black values common to these children seem inferior by comparison. The speeches of the professional city workers were emotionally charged and stirred an intense reaction among the listeners. The animosity against white people rose to a fevered pitch, and then something happened that changed everything.

A middle-aged black woman stood in the back of the room and asked a question: "You keep on talking about white middle-class values," she said. "What are these white middle-class values? I would like to know exactly what they are; you see, I never had the educational advantages that you city workers have had, so you've got to educate me, you've got to teach me."

There was a long pause, and, in the absence of any response from the city workers who were conducting the meeting, she went on. "Do you mean by white middle-class values that children would dress and talk like ladies and gentlemen? Do you mean that they will take school seriously, instead of playing basketball till one o'clock in the morning on the city playgrounds? By white middle-class values do you mean that you would have a two-car garage with two cars parked in it? That you would have a husband and a wife living together and that you have regular jobs? Do you mean by white middle-class values that you expect your children to go off to college? Is this what you mean by white middle-class values? Or do you mean something else?"

Dead silence filled the room. Then this woman went on to ask another question: "Well, if you can't tell me what white middle-class values are, could you please explain to me what black lower-class values are?"

Again there was dead silence, to which the woman responded. "Well, if you can't give me any answers to these questions then I can only say this: If white middle-class values are what I think they are, I say bring them on. I hope my children learn these values and what's more, I don't think they are white middle-class values, I just think they are the values of decent citizens."

Her speech changed everything. The meeting was adjourned. The EAPE program continued throughout the summer, and the families being served by it showed even greater enthusiasm and appreciation for what the white university volunteers were doing than before.

Likewise, the white Christian community, particularly in the Evangelical tradition, maintains a very politically and socially conservative worldview that puts a great emphasis on personal responsibility. White Christians tend to believe that African American people too readily blame white society for all of their troubles. Some might say that this demonstrates the blame-the-victim mentality of modern racism, while others would say that they are pointing out the blame-the-system mentality of internalized racism. Yet the point remains that when black people are not around, white people are more likely to note that their black brothers and sisters have not taken advantage of the vast array of opportunities that have become available to them since the days of the Civil Rights movement.

When black people are not around white people are more likely to note that their black brothers and sisters have not taken advantage of the vast array of opportunities that have become available to them since the days of the civil rights movement.

African American religious thinker Cornel West argues that this is one critique black people cannot ignore.[7] He contends that while American society has not done nearly enough to create equal opportunities for African Americans, too many black people have failed to take advantage of the opportunities that are available to them, maintaining that American social structures violate the dignity of black people. A significant portion of the African American population readily refuses to embrace options for social improvement. The reasons for this refusal need to be explored. Moreover, African American people must be challenged, especially by members of their own community, to take advantage of the opportunities that are increasingly available within the American social system. Individual achievement cannot be ignored, especially in these years when white Evangelicals, with their heightened emphasis on such achievement, have become a powerful cultural and political force in America. In the atmosphere being generated by the religious right, more and more will be expected of individuals, and the white religious establishment will be less and less inclined to accept blame for the social privations and economic sufferings that exist in the black community.

One sign of both the promise and problems of such intra-community accountability can be seen in the controversy stirred up by comedian Bill Cosby in 2004 when, in a speech before the NAACP, he criticized the lifestyles of black young people. He specifically took aim at their language, in which profanity and obscenities regularly punctuated their conversations. He also went on to criticize the rap music that had become a dominant mode of entertainment, particularly among black young people. He cited lyrics that depict the sexual exploitation of women and violence in a cavalier manner, which gives such antisocial behavior a significant degree of social legitimacy. Some black leaders criticized Cosby, contending that his comments would only support the prejudicial attitudes that white people express when they talk about blacks in private. While it is difficult to evaluate that contention, what is notable is that a host of prominent African American spokespersons stepped forward to lend support to Cosby's remarks.

Even as Cosby, West, and others try to promote such personal responsibility for social problems in the African American community, the Christian community, both black and white, has struggled to address such issues helpfully. The legacies of racism, contemporary attitudes of political correctness, and the race-based identity that has trumped baptismal identity among Christians have prevented too many Christians from being able to speak the truth in love when it comes to matters of racial reconciliation, leaving them mired in the politics of resignation and the church still enslaved.

CHAPTER 4

Racist Myths
and Taboos

*Some of our most pervasive attitudes are rooted in
centuries-old myths about race, body, and sexuality*

When talking about race and racism in contemporary America, it is inevitable that the conversation will turn to the dire situation of young African American men, particularly in urban situations. The statistics are staggering: The U.S. Bureau of Justice Statistics estimates that 30 percent of twelve-year-old African American boys will spend time in jail in their lifetimes—far more than will attend college. Moreover, because of laws that deny convicted felons the right to vote, an estimated 13 percent of all black men, including one in every three in Alabama and Florida, cannot participate in the electoral process. Across the country, incarceration rates for African Americans have greatly surpassed those for whites.

These sorts of numbers contribute to an overwhelming sense of anger among many African American men, which in turn has created a host of social problems, not least of which is the "unemployability" of black men—a key factor in the breakdown of African American families. These factors further exacerbate self-defeating behaviors and self-hatred among African Americans that keep too many mired in the byproducts of racist structures and attitudes. This black self-hatred deserves closer scrutiny for the many complex issues that play into it.

The Mind–Body Dichotomy

In the heyday of the Black Power movement, former Black Panther Eldridge Cleaver, in his book *Soul on Ice*, expressed the enduring insight that racism is, in part, related to a philosophical tradition that goes all the way back to the time of the ancient Greeks.[1] According to Cleaver, it was the Greeks who developed the mind–body dichotomy. That is, the ancient Greek understanding of human nature was that what is intellectual and spiritual about human beings is good, and what is physical and material is evil. According to this view, human beings are spiritual entities imprisoned in physical bodies that smother and oppress their spiritual essence.

> *Since the physical has been deemed inferior to the intellectual-spiritual side of human nature, the white race has always been willing to assign superiority to blacks when it comes to physical matters, while reserving spiritual-intellectual superiority for itself.*

We see this dichotomy even in the New Testament, where Paul talks about the lust of the flesh on the one hand and the fruits of the spirit on the other. From the very beginning, Greek thinking permeated and distorted Christianity and at times almost obliterated its Hebraic roots of symmetry and balance. Jews did not have the kind of negative disposition toward the physical aspects of life, nor did they see the human body as a source of evil. Rather, Jews saw that all that God created was good, while Greeks set forth a worldview in which there was only a negative judgment against physical human existence.

Cleaver argues that the way this mind–body dichotomy has worked itself out in race relationships whites, usually being willing to assign superiority to blacks when it comes to physical matters, while reserving spiritual-intellectual superiority for themselves. Even worse, according to Cleaver, black people themselves have readily accepted this dualistic perception of the differences between whites and blacks, in particular the assertion that black people are physically superior.

If you gather a group of African Americans together and simply ask, "Do you think that blacks are better athletes than whites?" you know what the answer would be: "Of course!" They will rightly point out that all you have to do is look at the players on the court in the NBA, or look at the lineups of football players in the NFL, and even consider the players in Major League Baseball. You will see an overwhelming preponderance of blacks, not only in the make-up of the teams but also playing at the top of their respective games when it comes to physical ability and achievement. This evidence, they would claim, speaks for itself. They state further that there is a common charge made in basketball that "white men can't jump." Similarly, it is also commonly accepted that black athletes at the Olympics will always run faster than white athletes.

The Racism
of Physical Superiority Myths

What often is not perceived when black people affirm their physical superiority is that at the same time they are subtly ascribing intellectual superiority to white people. Tony reports that he sees this going on in the lives of students at Eastern University, where he taught for more than 38 years. White students expect that their black colleagues will do better on the basketball team, whereas black students expect that their white friends will do better in the classroom. Black students coming out of predominantly black high schools in Philadelphia to Eastern University, which is located in the suburbs of that city, come with a distinct sense of intellectual inferiority. Tony reports that getting black students through the first year of their studies was a Herculean task. They come into the classroom convinced that white students are smarter than they are and that they won't be able to compete. It takes them at least a year to realize that the

> *What often is not perceived when black people affirm their physical superiority is that at the same time they are subtly ascribing intellectual superiority to white people.*

whites are no smarter than they are and that they are quite capable of keeping up. Overcoming the prejudices that come from an *a priori* assumption that intellectual activity is a "white thing" and that physical activity is a "black thing" is a slow process for these African American students. And, as already noted in chapter 3, this sort of prejudice often takes root early in the education process and results in harassment for black children who attempt to break through these stereotypes.

On the other hand, when it comes to taking to the basketball court, white players at Eastern University were usually intimidated by the presence of black players. Tony, himself a basketball player during his college days, reports that he never did well in the beginning of a game when he was guarded by a black player. He acknowledges that it would take him at least ten minutes to forget the race of his opponent and simply get on with playing the game. Yet it is interesting to note that a significant number of white players from Europe are entering the NBA these days and challenging African American players. Could it be that European whites are not as brainwashed by their culture into believing that they are unable to compete with blacks in athletic events and thus are able to play without intimidation, whereas American whites readily buy into the mind–body dichotomy?

There will be those, both black and white, who will argue for the superiority of black athletes and claim they really are superior when it comes to physical activities. Increasingly, however, even these voices are somewhat stunned when the Olympic basketball "dream teams" made up of highly paid black professionals from the NBA have been losing to white teams from other countries during the games, such as in 2004, when Latvia beat the U.S.A. team. Many feel the same way when a white, blonde-haired, blue-eyed German beats out an African American sprinter and middle-distance runner. We continually tell ourselves that white men can't jump and then are a bit perplexed when white men beat out American blacks in the high jump and the pole vault.

Basketball star Julius "Dr. J" Erving was once asked whether or not blacks were really better athletes than whites. He wisely answered:

It's hard to say. Black kids start playing basketball when they're eight or nine years old and play several hours every day. At the same time, white parents are making their children study. White children are reading books while black children are throwing balls through hoops. So who can say when they reach the age of 18 or 19 that it's a matter of the genes that make black athletes so successful and white students such achievers?[2]

The Racism of Beauty Myths

The mind–body dichotomy Cleaver described takes on yet more complexity when one considers his battle cry, "Black is beautiful," words that empowered millions of African American people to look at themselves in new ways after years of having their appearances caricatured and made the butt of racist jokes. Yet, nearly forty years after that initial groundbreaking pronouncement, it behooves us to ask, Is black still beautiful? The answer is no.

It is about time we faced this reality. The answer should be yes, but it is no. When a black woman wins a beauty contest, she often wins because she looks white. She does not have African physical characteristics: she wears straight hair, her body form is European, her skin tone is light.

Cornel West traces this philosophically to the European sense of beauty, a concept of beauty that also came from the ancient Greeks.[3] According to West, when Western culture emerged from the Renaissance, it espoused everything Hellenistic. Thus, Greek philosophers molded Western understandings about thought, education, lifestyle, and standards of beauty (as epitomized by the statue of Venus de Milo). Through this Greek goddess of beauty, Westerners were given an ideal form and body that told them what all bodies should try to approximate. As the Western world took over Africa, it imposed on the Africans Western concepts and images of beauty to which black people have been trying to measure up ever since.

As noted in chapter 1, Malcolm X tells in his autobiography how, as a child, he tried to straightened his air with irons. He also recounts there how everybody in Harlem was trying to look white. When children were born in black families, it was the lighter-skinned children who ended up being the favorites. So the Greek concept of beauty permeated not only the sensibilities of Europeans, who could conform to it, but also those of black people, who could not—at least not without extreme effort and artificial means.

So while both blacks and whites continue to assert that black is beautiful, deep down inside, both communities seem to be saying still, "Black is ugly." This sense of self-hatred in the black community is a deep problem. Black people *learned* to hate black people.

This problem of self-hatred is not common only with black people in the United States. In China, India, Eastern Europe, and many other places around the world, darker complexions are also thought of as being ugly. For instance, Michael's Chinese roommate in graduate school told him that many Chinese people carry umbrellas to prevent the hot sun from tanning their bodies so as not to appear like a peasant who works the fields. Ironically, many white people in America crave darker skin and spend millions of dollars every year to achieve deep tans through various means both natural and artificial, even at the risk of skin cancer in some cases. Pale skin is generally looked down upon for white celebrities and business people, while a well-maintained tan declares one's higher status and health.

Yet many societies still tend to favor those who have lighter skin. And when it comes to beauty contests the physical make-up of the winners is usually attuned to white, Western standards of attractiveness in body shape (slim waists and hips are in; more full-figured qualities are taboo), hair style and color (straight and blonde is preferable to black afros), and facial features (small noses and thin lips are acceptable; more traditionally African qualities are not). Both white *and* black Miss America contestants are expected to meet these standards. This Western standard of beauty continues to pervade the black consciousness.

Malcolm X talked about the need to overcome the desire to look white because such a desire is an inculcation of a hatred toward what it means to be a black person. Therefore, blacks themselves have unconsciously absorbed from the dominant culture an inherent racism. It would seem that Malcolm X's pleadings have failed to overcome this desire that it is alive and well in the black community today, demonstrated

Although both blacks and whites continue to assert that black is beautiful, deep down inside both communities seem to be saying still, "Black is ugly."

most radically, perhaps, by the pop star Michael Jackson, who has erased most of his black features through extensive plastic surgery and skin bleaching. Yet Malcolm was on the right track when he affirmed the need for blacks to have their own aesthetics. Still, the black community seems to be far from achieving that at the present time. It is one of the important realities that have to be addressed if racism is to be eliminated. Blacks must not only come up with their own definitions of what it means to be beautiful but they must be able to teach the white community to recognize *how* black is beautiful.

The Racism of Sexual Superiority Myths

The most serious consequence of the mind–body dichotomy we inherited from the ancient Greek worldview is that sex is solely a physical activity. Those who believe that blacks are superior to whites in all things physical will also ascribe sexual superiority to blacks. Racism, therefore, is filled with sexual overtones. For example, black men are often viewed as insatiable sexual creatures. Many black men themselves nurture that image, saying that if white women ever experienced sex with a black man, they would never want to have sex with a white man again. Myths about black sexuality have led to a host of racial barriers in which whites lack sexuality and blacks are merely sexual creatures. Even today many express fears that black men have a serious appetite for white women and that white women find black men irresistible, perpetuating the myth of black male physical superiority that further perverts realistic perceptions across racial lines. Such fears are particularly acute among black women who see few good marriage prospects among black men, and thus feel threatened when white women and black men date or marry each other. Greek philosophers, according to Cleaver, have really done a job on us all!

Cleaver came to these conclusions regarding the mind–body dichotomy as he studied and reflected during a prison term he served for raping a white woman. While in prison he put up a centerfold from *Playboy* magazine on the wall of this cell, which enraged one of the white guards, who ripped it down and said to Cleaver, "If you want to put something up on the wall, why don't you get a black woman?" At first, Cleaver was filled with anger and resentment, but then he began to ask himself why he put up a picture of a white woman in the first place. Why didn't he have a picture of a black woman there?

As he asked other black men in prison whom they preferred as sex partners, he found that over and over again their answer was white women. One of his black prison mates told him, "The only thing I want black is my Cadillac." Cleaver thought through what his black brothers in prison told him about their preference for white women and asked why this was the case. After all, if, according to the myth, whites are physically inferior, then it would stand to reason that white women would then be less desirable sexual partners. But the myth of black physical superiority has caused many white women to believe that black men are extra special in bed; this leads to a special turn-on among these women, which is exciting for black men as well. Second, his conversations convinced him that, for many of these men, having a white woman as a sexual partner is a way of getting back at white people. He heard his black brothers talk about the sense of satisfaction they gained when they walked

> *Racism is filled with sexual overtones. Black men are often viewed as insatiable sexual creatures.*

down the street with a white, blond-haired, blue-eyed woman in tow. They talked about the enjoyment they took in seeing resentment on the faces of white men who looked upon them with envy. There was a sense among his black brothers that by dating white women they were getting back at the white man, taking his most precious possession.

The mind–body dichotomy has also played itself out in relations between black women and white men, though in different ways. Psychologist and social scientist John Dollard's classic book, *Caste and Class in a Southern Town*, used psychological theories to analyze the interaction between blacks and whites in a south Georgia community in the early part of the twentieth century.[4] With careful observations, Dollard described how white men preyed on black women for sexual favors, viewing them as sexual objects with voracious erotic appetites. Many of the women whom they sexually exploited were poor women who made themselves available to white oppressors out of their need for money to support their children.

Embracing the Freudian concept of the defensive mechanism of projection, Dollard stated that white men of this community sought women in the black community as objects and projected onto black men the sin of which they themselves were guilty. In other words, while they were after black women as sexual objects, they projected this motive and became convinced that black men were after "their" women.

Making this complex situation even more explosive, said Dollard, was that the white women in this community were sometimes sexually neglected, given that the sexual energies of these white men were dissipated in their encounters with black women, and given the prevailing attitudes denying white women sexual pleasure. Thus, many of the white women ended up with unsatisfied sexual desires and turned their fantasies toward affairs with black men, again, fueled by the basic myth that black men were incredible sexual partners. Dollard substantiated this theoretical framework through interviews that constitute the bulk of his study.

Harper Lee's famous novel, *To Kill a Mockingbird*—later an equally popular and acclaimed movie starring Gregory Peck—dramatizes this theme.[5] In that story, a sexually frustrated white woman propositions a black man, and when he rejects her advances, she seeks to destroy him out of fear that her indiscretion might be exposed by claiming that he tried to rape her. Given the sexually charged atmosphere of the southern town in which the story is set, the community is ready to condemn the black man to death simply on the basis of the accusation. It should be noted that lynching black men without a trial was common under the accusation of rape. Such an accusation by a white woman against a black man—or even the suggestion thereof—could result in a lynching. Herein one gains the sense of deep sexual fears that white men had about the physical prowess of black men; and it should be noted that in case after case black men who were lynched were also castrated. All of the above suggests that racism is not just a sociological problem; there is also a psychological pathology nurtured by cultural factors.

Clergy on both the white and black sides of the racial divide are particularly afraid to deal with racism when it means also having to consider sexual overtones, which have such a psychological onus connected to them. Too often, clergy would rather go along as though all that is necessary to overcome racism is for black people and white people to get to know each other and spend a little time in fellowship. If we can just cross our arms and hold each other hands and sing a few verses of "We Shall Overcome" more frequently, they think, somehow the complex psychological tensions that exist between blacks and whites will disappear. Obviously, much more is needed. It is essential that racism be studied in all of its dimensions, even those that make us most uncomfortable.

> *Racial prejudice is bathed in pathological sexual overtones that need to be dealt with by church leaders.*

When racism is discussed in contemporary congregations, it is usually expressed in terms of economic factors and issues of racial discrimination in the marketplace, as we did in the beginning of this chapter. Yet leaders of the church seldom will dare even to approach the kind of subject matter discussed immediately above. Nevertheless, racial prejudice is bathed in pathological, sexual overtones that need to be dealt with by church leaders. They need to air out the truth and find the healing that comes from confession and healing the Holy Spirit. The church has a lot of therapeutic work to do if it is to be free and to live out the call of Christ that we all might be one. In the next two chapters we look more closely at some of those uncomfortable pathologies—as well as strengths—that continue to have an impact on how both black and white churches deal with the complexities of racism.

CHAPTER 5

Challenges for White Churches

America's white churches, especially evangelical churches, need to take a hard look at their past and present racism.

W
e have already made the case that racism and racial separation continue to prevail in the white church. Too often white churches are complicit with the politics of resignation that either ignores or avoids the complexities of racism. Yet the problem is neither as monolithic as it might first appear nor is it as hopeless. For instance, it is important to note distinct differences in how such racism is expressed in white Evangelical churches in comparison to so-called mainline Protestant denominations, such as the Presbyterian Church–USA (PCUSA), the Episcopal Church, the United Church of Christ, the United Methodist Church, or the Evangelical Lutheran Church in America. Nearly all denominations in the latter category have long had antiracism initiatives, at least on the national level. Many of these denominations' leaders were active in the Civil Rights movement in the 1960s and this legacy has been carried forward in subsequent generations. In addition, many of these denominations regularly issue social statements and policy directives that express opposition to structural evils in both the United States and abroad (such as opposition to South African apartheid or, more recently, PCUSA's controversial divestment from Israeli businesses in protest of Palestinian oppression). Such efforts also illustrate the middle-of-the-road to liberal political views that have often been connected with

the Protestant mainline, views that many observers say partially account for these denominations' membership losses since their heyday in the 1950s.

While the Protestant mainline remains overwhelmingly white in its overall racial make-up, there are strong signs that racial reconciliation efforts are at the forefront of the agendas for many individual faith communities. Episcopal theologian Sheryl Kujawa-Holbrook, in her book *A House of Prayer for All People*, has chronicled seven mainline Protestant congregations that exemplify not only local efforts to work for racial reconciliation but also demonstrate how individual churches can give substance to and take leadership on such measures. Although the history of race relations in such mainline denominations remains mixed at best, Kujawa-Holbrook's work suggests that such grassroots efforts at racial reconciliation may show the most promise to have transforming effects on national church structures.[1]

Evangelicalism's Complicity with Racism

The legacy of racism and racial reconciliation in white Evangelical churches, however, is much more problematic and deserves special consideration. Since the middle of the 1950s, one can easily trace Evangelicalism's complicity with racism. In response to the Supreme Court's school desegregation ruling in 1954, a massive number of Southern Baptist churches started their own Christian schools designed explicitly for whites alone. Since that time, and to their credit, many of these one-time exclusively segregated Christian academies have opened themselves to receive black students. Moreover, many of them even offer scholarship aid to poor black families who cannot afford to send their children to these schools. Nevertheless, the message was clearly

The message was clearly sounded that Southern Baptist churches were committed to conservative social policies that militated against racial integration.

sounded that these churches were committed to conservative social policies that militated against racial integration. In fact, during the Civil Rights era, many white Evangelical churches became bastions of white segregationist attitudes. In many cases, black people were barred from membership and even from worship.

The statements and policy declarations of many Evangelical churches and leaders provide a revealing contrast to the measures taken by mainline Protestant churches. It was common in Evangelical circles to label Martin Luther King Jr. a communist. Evangelical publications like *Christianity Today* portrayed civil rights demonstrations as rabble-rousing and called King a troublemaker. In the same way, when Nelson Mandela was living the struggle to end apartheid in South Africa, Evangelical preachers Jerry Falwell and Pat Robertson both openly sided with the forces that opposed Mandela and labeled him and his supporters, like King, as communists. Falwell went so far as to call South African Archbishop Desmond Tutu a "phony."

These stances among Evangelical leaders often directly reflect the platform of the Republican Party and the assertions of political conservatives. If liberalism is the ideology that forced a way for equality, it easily can be said that, for Evangelicals, being politically liberal is a bad thing. Indeed, it seems that Evangelicalism has become married to the Republican Party. This became blatantly evident during and following the 2004 presidential election, when at least 83 percent of self-avowed Evangelicals voted for George W. Bush and allied themselves with the policies of his party. Bush had already raised the eyebrows of many African American leaders by taking a stand against affirmative action. The appointment to the Civil Rights Commission of a black chairman who was avowedly opposed to affirmative action sent a strong signal as to how President Bush and many in his party regarded this policy. In short, given the political allegiances of the Evangelical church in the Bible Belt, particularly within the southern states, it is not surprising that such positions became widely spread throughout the Evangelical world.

The Evangelical Emphasis
on Individualism

One can decipher some theological roots among Evangelicals that support the Republican Party's opposition to affirmative action. All Evangelicals are not necessarily rac-ists, but many may be caught up in a self-defeating worldview. For exam-ple, given the intense opposition that Evangelicals have expressed toward evolutionary theory, careful analy-sis of Evangelical beliefs and thinking demonstrates that, in the end, they are

> *Many evangelicals have a tendency to see sin only in individualistic terms, and it is hard to convince them that there is such a thing as structural evil.*

social Darwinists. That is, they apply the "survival of the fittest" dictum to individual personal behavior, meaning that political and social policy should favor those in society who have the best means to thrive within the existing system. This strong emphasis on indi-vidualism in Evangelicalism is not surprising given their attitudes towards personal salvation as provided through Jesus Christ. They have a tendency to see sin only in individualistic terms and it is hard to convince them that there is such a thing as structural, or systemic, evil. One evangelical seminary professor even told Tony once that he and his seminary colleagues did not believe in such a thing as structural evil and that such an idea is nothing more than a liberal concoction.

This emphasis on individualism is a root cause of the failure in the Evangelical community to deal with systemic racism. The prowess of evangelicals is to save individual souls and their weak-ness is to let principalities and powers run amok in the meantime. We assert that a counteremphasis on Jesus's true religion and call to be an emancipated church is the best way to address this problem of individualism.

Not only is sin understood in individualistic terms for many white Evangelicals, but all goodness is the result of individual deci-sion making. For instance, those who buy into the doctrine of social Darwinism believe that efforts to provide safety nets for people who are not making it in society prove counterproductive to the good of society in the long run. When government programs only perpetuate the number of unfit people who reproduce and have children, say social Darwinists, then they can only become additional burdens to society. Social Darwinists such as Franklin H. Giddons have argued with great effectiveness that the government that does the least to help "the unfit members of society" is probably the government that fosters optimum social progress. Only when the unfit fade away through neglect will they become productive in society and make things better for all. This aggressive neglect is a subtle yet distinct contrast to the benign neglect advocated by Daniel Moynihan, yet it may be the inevitable extension of Moynihan's policy as well. Rugged individualism, given this philosophy, is the way to go; consequently, those who affirm this mind-set find themselves opposed to all those government programs aimed at providing extra help for those who seem to have been left behind as America has progressed onward and upward to greater well-being and economic prosperity.

Recently the educational policies promoted by President George W. Bush under the aegis of "No Child Left Behind" gives evidence of this social Darwinist mind-set and value system. Under the auspices of the Department of Education, a program of testing has been instituted for students across America. When the students of a particular school fall below acceptable levels of their academic success, federal grants are denied to their schools as punishment. On the other hand, those schools that do very well will get additional financial support from the government. Clearly, such policies favor well-financed school systems in mostly white, suburban neighborhoods, while underfunded and crumbling schools in mostly black, urban neighborhoods will suffer. Here we have social Darwinism enacted through modern social and educational policies.

> *A heightened sense of individualism nurtured by latent social Darwinist's ideology, has produced among Evangelicals an attitude that all that is right and wrong in people's lives is due to personal responsibility.*

Once, as Tony was attending worship in a black church, the pastor read the parable of the talents from Matthew 25:14-29, which ends with Jesus saying, "For unto everyone that hath shall be given, and he shall have abundance: but from him that hath not shall be taken away even that which he hath." Upon the conclusion of the reading of that verse, Tony heard an African American woman sitting behind him mumble, "Don't tell me those people in Washington don't read the Bible!"

In summary, a heightened sense of individualism nurtured by latent social Darwinist ideology, has produced among Evangelicals an attitude that whatever is right and wrong in people's lives is due to personal responsibility. On one hand, such an ideology ignores the impact of social forces that hinder certain people from ever succeeding; and on the other hand, such an ideology creates the illusion that those who do succeed owe their success to their superior character traits. It is easy to see how this kind of thinking can support a racist attitude that views the plight of black people as the result of their particular inadequacies—the modern racism category of blaming the victim we discussed in chapter 1. Those who think this way love to point out individual African Americans who have succeeded by pulling themselves up by their bootstraps, and cite them as examples of what every black person should be able to do. Such an ideology pervades Evangelical churches, and it needs to be studied, critiqued, and challenged. This does not negate our earlier point that black people must acknowledge that they as individuals are capable of achieving a great deal, given the opportunities that are presently available to them in America. Yet it does reveal a tension with the reality that there are still social forces at work in America that keep African American people in oppressed situations and that racial discrimination still operates subtlely and effectively—and structurally.

Connections between racist religious organizations and the Republican Party are slowly being exposed, and some progress can be detected. During the 2000 Republican primaries, schools that have had openly racist policies, like Bob Jones University in South Carolina, became notorious. Improvements have been made, but

Bob Jones University, as well as a host of other Evangelical schools, have a long way to go before things are set right. In the same way, *Christianity Today* magazine has come a long way in recent years in both its attitudes and its policies.

African Americans and the Southern Baptist Convention

The unusual phenomenon worth noting here is the formation, over the last few years, of surprising new relationships between black Christians and the Southern Baptist Convention. As noted above, during the Civil Rights era, Southern Baptists lent very little support, and often a great deal of opposition to, civil rights leaders like Martin Luther King Jr.; kept black people from even worshiping in their churches; and helped create all-white Christian academies in the South in response to desegregation court rulings. It was only a few years ago that the Southern Baptist Convention, at one of its annual meetings, confessed its sin of racism and asked forgiveness from the black community. Despite this history of racism, a significant number of African American churches have joined up with the Southern Baptist Convention in the last few years, much to the chagrin of groups like the National Baptist Convention and the Progressive Baptist Convention, two of the largest black denominations in the United States.

The reasons behind these new affiliations are easily discernable. First and foremost, the Southern Baptist Convention offers to black pastors a retirement program that is superior to anything they might gain within black denominations. The leaders of the Southern Baptist Convention and these black pastors alike can easily play a game of denial on this matter. Yet there is no doubt that the annuity plan offered by the Southern Baptists has played a major role in bringing black pastors and their churches into the Southern Baptist fold.

Second, the Southern Baptist Convention is making significant financial resources available to black congregations, who often are in desperate need of such resources. It has the ability to provide financial undergirding for the creation of inner-city social programs, youth tutoring programs, and economic development programs that many African American churches desperately need to sustain their ministries. Such resources are often not otherwise available to these churches.

Third, Southern Baptists were once the fastest-growing denomination in America, but within the last few years they have experienced a slight decline in membership. This is largely due to fundamentalist takeover, which has left many of the key churches and some of the formerly loyal members extremely alienated. By getting black churches to change their affiliation and join the Southern Baptist Convention, they have generated the illusion that their membership is a lot healthier than it really is. Thus, the denomination gets a significant payoff for its investment as it lures black congregations into its membership.

> *There is no doubt that the annuity plan offered by the Southern Baptists has played a major role in bringing black pastors and their churches into the Southern Baptist fold.*

Obviously, there is much to criticize about this alliance between black congregations and the Southern Baptist Convention. But it may prove to have transformative effects on Evangelicalism at large, just as individual congregations' antiracism efforts are beginning to transform mainstream Protestantism. In an America split along red state/blue state lines, along liberal/conservative ideological fault lines, we may well be witnessing signs of hope in the very organizations that so discourage and divide millions of Americans, both black and white.

Evangelical Sources
for Countering Racism

Indeed, there are many sources within Evangelical theology that counter this hyperindividualism and point to ways of addressing systemic evil and defeating the racism in our midst. The late Dutch

Reformed theologian Hendrik Berkhof, in his seminal book *Christ and the Powers*, points out that the apostle Paul refers to structural evil when he wrote about principalities and powers.[2] Berkhof makes the case that all principalities and powers (that is, social forces) were created by God and ordained for the good of all of God's children; however, because of the Fall, these powers come under the influence of the "evil one." Instead of doing the good they were intended to do, often these powers become instruments of destruction. In Ephesians 6:12, we are called upon to wrestle with these principalities and powers and bring them into submission to the will of God. According to Berkhof, Paul makes the case in Ephesians 1:19-23 that these powers can be challenged and brought into submission to God through a faithful church. This is the calling of the body of Christ: not to be enslaved by "principalities and powers." Paul's insights help us all to deal more effectively with social, economical, and political systems that foster racism:

> With the eyes of your heart enlightened, you may know . . . what is the immeasurable greatness of this power for us who believe, according to the working of his great power. God put this power to work in Christ when he raised him from the dead and seated him at his right hand in the heavenly places, far above all rule and authority and power and dominion, and above every name that is named, not only in this age but also in the age to come. And he has put all things under his feet and has made him the head over all things for the church, which is his body, the fullness of him who fills all in all. (Ephesians 1:18-23)

Praying against demonic spirits is something only extreme Pentecostals can do, especially when it comes to the spirits inherent in social structures. Spiritual warfare must become part of the church of Jesus Christ as it stands against structural evil. We not only must learn to pray against evil forces but also, when we enter into the struggle to change the system, we must do so fully equipped with the armor of Christ, as described by Ephesians 6:12-18.

Make no mistake: Evangelicals take evil seriously. Therefore, all people need to see the evil of racism. Consider the story of spiritual writer William Stringfellow when he was engaged in civil rights struggles as a lawyer working in Harlem. The mistakes he made in his work were characterized by not taking demonic forces seriously. In his popular book, *An Ethic for Christians and Other Aliens in a Strange Land,* Stringfellow showed that, in his naïveté, he thought setting things right in racial matters required only electing good people to positions of power to replace those he thought were bad people.[3] He said that he and his colleagues failed to see that an evil intelligence behind those who propagated evil policies was in control of things, whose power permeated the social systems in which policy makers lived and did their work. Because they did not confront those demonic forces, but ignored their existence, Stringfellow felt that much of their work ended up being futile.

> *Spiritual warfare must become part of the church of Jesus Christ as it stands against structural evil.*

Such thinking may be strange to many of our readers, but in a postmodern world where Western rationalism is seriously called into question, an understanding of evil spirits manipulating social systems to the detriment of humanity is no longer outlandish. To deal with racism we need to develop a strategy for spiritual warfare not only on an individualistic level but on a societal level as well. In some ways, as we will see in the next chapter, black churches are neither immune to such individualism nor attuned to systemic evil. Yet it is also undeniable that within the many forms that the black church takes, there are other sources that may point the way to a more prophetic stance on race issues among Evangelicals and opportunities to bridge this white and black spiritual separation.

CHAPTER 6

Challenges for Black Churches

The powerful black-church legacy needs to be understood—and also reformed

The black church in the United States has taken forms that are unique to its character as a community of believers born out of oppression and white hegemony. As noted in chapter 2, during the days of slavery the white overlords in the South were afraid of allowing black people to have their own churches, lest they develop leadership networks that could foment rebellion or facilitate escape. In the North, however, free blacks did organize their own congregations. Philadelphia's famous Mother Bethel Church, presided over by Bishop Richard Allen and the first African Methodist Episcopal church in the United States, became a center for African American Christianity. Out of that church, a host of other congregations were spun out across the nation, creating worshiping communities specifically for African American people. When slavery was ended, it did not take long for blacks to establish their own congregations in the South for their own preachers, and soon black denominations grew up linking black churches together. Today, black Christianity flourishes from one end of the country to the other in thousands of African American congregations.

It is far too easy to criticize the separation of blacks and whites in American church life without acknowledging anything positive about it. One example is what even critics of this racial separation have always recognized: all-black congregations have nurtured black leadership within their walls. Throughout the history of the Civil Rights movement in the United States, and even today, the black church has been the center of formation for many of the leaders we now celebrate such as Martin Luther King Jr., Jesse Jackson, and Al Sharpton. These prominent clergymen have given voice to the grave issues and concerns of the African American community and have become prophetic instruments who speak truth to the power establishments that keep white people in the role of oppressors. For sociocultural reasons, many blacks tended to defer to the leadership of whites in most social settings, especially when whites are present in significant numbers. In the face of this denigrating deference, however, the leaders of the Black Separatist movement made it clear that, at least in the short run, black people needed to separate themselves from the white community until they had developed the security and self-assurance necessary to engage whites as equals.

> *It is within that historical context of separation during slavery, after slavery, and the Civil Rights movement that the black church took the shapes that distinguish it today.*

It is within that historical context of separation during slavery, after slavery, and the Civil Rights movement that the black church took the shapes that distinguish it today. While there is yet to be developed a comprehensive typology for black churches, nevertheless some generalizations can be made, specifically three readily identifiable forms: (1) the storefront church, (2) the black megachurch, and (3) the denominational mainline church. While some might point to parallel forms among white churches, we believe that, examined through the aforementioned historical framework and the attendant theological thought that emerged from those circumstances, these three forms take a distinct shape within the African American context that make them more dissimilar than similar to their white counterparts. In this chapter we will closely examine this "typology" of black churches, showing their significance to the African American community, their distinctiveness compared to the white church, the weaknesses that hold them back from building bridges with the white church, and the gifts that these churches have to offer to the church at large.

The Storefront Church

Perhaps the most common type of black church, but also the least understood and appreciated, is the *storefront church*. Often, these congregations are pastored by self-appointed clergy who, due to their personal charisma, are able to attract small followings. These preachers base their authority to preach and lead in these storefront churches by claiming to have a special calling from God. Once when Tony asked a storefront preacher whether he had any plans to go on to seminary for education, the preacher responded, "No way. When those seminaries finish with you, there's not enough power to preach the fuzz off of a peach." This preacher continued, "I have a calling from God and I've got the Holy Spirit as a teacher and I don't really need anything else." In especially poor neighborhoods in urban settings, storefront churches seem omnipresent. Five such congregations have meeting places within one city block in the neighborhood where Tony grew up in west Philadelphia; similar situations of close proximity can be found in Washington, D. C., Atlanta, New York, and numerous other cities.[1] None of these congregations draws more than fifty people to worship, and the pastors in almost every case are bivocational; only by having a non-church-related job are they able to earn a living.

The worship services in storefront churches tend to be emotionally charged and characterized by rhythmic singing of well-known black gospel songs. Prosperity theology marks the sermons, with an aim to convince the listeners that if they do the right thing according to Scripture, God will bless them in social and material ways. This is coupled with a strong emphasis on tithing. Preachers exhort their congregants to do "what's right" and set aside 10 percent of their income for the church. They tell congregants that such offerings will ensure that God will bless them with financial and familial well-being.

Along with tithing and prosperity theology, over the last few years there is increasing evidence of what can be called the "seed-promise theology." Put simply, this means that if one gives 10 percent "up front" to the church, God will make sure that the giver receives back a ninefold amount for their investment in the work of the church. Such economic practices represent what sociologists call a religio-magical dimension that has come to shape storefront Christianity.

Storefront churches have a strong emphasis on miracles that God can perform for the faithful, and testimonies to miraculous healings fill the worship services. God's miraculous intervention is often hoped for among the poor who lack the financial means to get the medical care they need. Healing services are often a specialty of these storefront churches. Prayer handkerchiefs, said to be imbued with magical capabilities, are sometimes offered to congregants in order to find their miracle from God.

Although many Christians find this emphasis on prosperity and healing to be theologically unsophisticated and even deceptive, it is far too easy to merely ridicule storefront churches and ignore the important role they have played in the black community. These congregations have long provided a vital transitional space for African American Christians who come out of southern rural settings seeking ways to integrate into the sophisticated and complex worlds of northern urban living. Especially during the great northern migration of the mid-twentieth century—when thousands of blacks fled the Jim Crow laws that dominated southern culture and the poverty resulting from diminishing job opportunities in the rural South—the storefront church provided a solace for those going through the pains of the extreme social disorientation that comes with such a move. For these northern migrants, storefront churches were reminiscent of those small, struggling, white clapboard churches that one can still readily find on the hilly back roads of North and South Carolina as well as other places in

> *Storefront churches provide a transition place that facilitates the movement of rural black people into the complicated world that typifies big-city life.*

the South. The kind of religion and the kind of worship expressed in the storefronts resembled closely what these black people left behind in the little churches back home. They heard the same kind of preaching with the same kind of emphasis and participated in the same kind of singing. Dislocation is always difficult to handle and, even today, when geographical shifts in employment opportunities occur constantly, the storefront churches provide a transition place that facilitates the movement of rural black people into the complicated world that typifies big-city life.

Storefront churches even maintain the kind of social life found in the rural communities whence many of their people came. These churches are like extended families and provide a place where people can enjoy life together. Tony recalls some African Americans who visited his large and well-established Baptist church in west Philadelphia, who after a couple of Sundays stopped coming to church and gave up being part of that congregation. When he later talked to these new urban immigrants and asked them why they stopped coming to worship, the woman of the household said, "I don't like your church because it doesn't even smell like church." That was a new one for Tony, so he pursued the matter by asking what she meant by that statement: "What is a real church supposed to smell like?" The woman answered, "A real church smells like chicken."

The woman went on to explain that she used to love it when she sat in the little church in the rural Georgia community she came from, singing and swaying to the music and smelling the chicken being cooked in the basement for the after-church meal. Such a smell created within her a wild anticipation that was a source of great joy. All during the service she could imagine what it would be like when the service would be over, when she and all of her friends would share a chicken dinner for a couple of hours into the afternoon.

That is the kind of intimacy and fellowship often found in the storefront church and in which new arrivals from the rural south find great solace and emotional support. These churches are able to offer a great sense of belonging and importance for each member of the congregation. In a church of less than fifty people, every member takes on more significance than what they would likely experience in the large mainline denominational churches that place a higher value on anonymity.

Storefront churches in black communities have provided a place of faithful discipleship to Christ. Instead of writing off storefront churches as irrelevant, mainline denominational leaders should recognize the good that these congregations can provide for their congregants. Rather than ignoring them, the large established congregations, both white and black, should be reaching out to offer a lending hand to these small storefront churches. They could use their abundant resources to help storefront congregations start daycare centers that would serve not only the members but also poor families in the neighborhood desperately in need of such services. In so doing they could improve the outreach of these congregations to the larger community.

> *Instead of writing off storefront churches as irrelevant, mainline denominational leaders should recognize the good that these congregations can provide for their congregants.*

Larger denominational churches could set up training programs to help these congregations develop the organizational skills necessary to establish smooth-running and ongoing ministries. In short, storefront churches should not be belittled, and ways should be found to encourage and enhance these congregations so that they can better serve their own people as well as the people who live in their immediate vicinity.

This raises the question: Are black Christians (or white Christians!) ashamed of this storefront heritage? Black theology needs to be engaged from the storefront perspective, lest the gap between black theology and the black church only worsen.[2] The survival of the church—both black and white—may well depend on how well we can learn from storefront churches, particularly in light of recent research by Philip Jenkins and others who are documenting the decline of white religion.[3]

The Megachurch Movement

At the other end of the spectrum from the storefront in our typology of black churches are the so-called *megachurches* that have arisen within the African American community. Most megachurches are independent of denominational affiliations and maintain a strong bent toward Pentecostalism. Significant healing ministries are often part of these megachurches, and their worship services are commonly broadcast via radio and television. But the most evident characteristic of black megachurches is the dynamism of the preaching there. Black preachers in general have mastered the art of communicating through enthusiastic presentations, which makes listening to their sermons a joy to the congregants.

> Black megachurches are so much a product of the dynamism of their preachers that people generally regard the church by the name of the pastor and often forget that the church itself has a name.

Their churches are so much a product of the dynamism of their preaching that people commonly regard the church by the name of the pastor and often forget that the church itself has a name.

Several preachers from these black megachurches have gained national recognition recently. Most notable among these is T. D. Jakes, who is in charge of a huge congregation (The Potter's House in Dallas) and an ever-expanding television ministry. As Jakes travels across the country, conducting special services and evangelistic crusades, hundreds of thousands of people pack the stadiums where he speaks. These endeavors have made him such a prominent speaker that he was featured on the cover of *Time* magazine as "America's greatest preacher"; some have identified him as "the next Billy Graham."

Another African American preacher whose church (Oak Cliff Bible Fellowship Church in Dallas) has gained wide recognition is Tony Evans, who heads a ministry called "The Urban Alternative." Evans rose to prominence through his appearances at rallies of the Promise Keepers organization, the most prominent Christian men's movement in America, which draws millions of white men to its gatherings. Promise Keeper members recognize Tony Evans as the organization's most prominent speaker, which has gained him attention from the white Evangelical community that few other African American preachers receive.

Aside from Jakes, Evans, and a few other African American preachers, little recognition has been given in the national religious media to black megachurches and their preachers. Even when publications like *Christianity Today* give attention to such churches and their preachers through feature articles, the white community takes little notice of it, especially in comparison to the degree that they regard white megachurches. Indeed, there are many black megachurches across the country but they seldom get much recognition beyond the communities in which they are located.

One such black megachurch is Deliverance Evangelistic Church in the Philadelphia area. Few people outside the black community are aware of this church, which on Sunday morning draws somewhere in the vicinity of 20,000 worshipers—and sometimes more than 25,000. It is larger than the world-famous Willow Creek Church near Chicago, pastored by Bill Hybels, a white man. When asked why he and his congregation weren't better known, the Reverend Benjamin Smith Sr., founding pastor of Deliverance Church, said, "White megachurches all over the country are written up in Christian magazines with white pastors attending all kinds of conferences suited more for white culture. I don't have time for that sort of thing. All of my time is consumed right here at home with my own people's needs. I need to be here all the time in order to keep things going; and that's exactly where I choose to be." When asked why he didn't write books and speak at Christian conferences around the world, thus gaining wider exposure, Smith reiterated, "It takes all my time and energy just to take care of my own flock here in Philadelphia, I haven't got time to do anything else."

Deliverance Church has a huge facility in north Philadelphia that takes up most of the grounds where Connie Mack stadium, the one-time home baseball stadium of the Phillies, once stood.

The church's outreach to its neighborhood is astounding, offering an extensive array of programs from housing units for the elderly to marriage counseling, drug rehabilitation, cultural enrichment, and economic development. It has created a shopping mall that gives jobs to many members of the congregation who had been previously unemployed. By providing stores and jobs in the community where few stores previously existed, they have boosted the area's economy.

Another intriguing example of a black megachurch is the Baptist Cathedral, which is located in Perth Amboy, New Jersey, and pastored by one of Tony's former students, Donald Hilliard. While a student at Eastern University, Bishop Hilliard majored in sociology, doing extensive research on the black Muslim movement in the Chicago area. He was fascinated by the ways in which the Nation of Islam had revitalized derelict neighborhoods there. He observed firsthand the way Louis Farrakhan's followers took over shuttered stores and businesses and made them functional once again, thus fostering wholistic redevelopment of these communities.

Hilliard endeavored to implement a similar program under the banner of Christ, which has proven to be incredibly successful. First, the church bought a large theater that once showed pornographic movies and turned it into a worship center. The church fixed up stores up and down Perth Amboy's main street and reopened them for business. These initiatives have given new vitality to a city that was close to total death. Hilliard's theological sophistication enables him to sift elements out of the Nation of Islam that will serve and benefit his own African American community. While he discards some teachings of the Nation of Islam that many deem racist and harmful to the future of black people in America, Dilliard is sensitive to the fact that Farrakhan's criticisms of white American Christianity must be taken seriously.

The size of black megachurches—and the huge amount of money they are able to attract into their coffers—obviously has many advantages for the black community. These churches are able to help spark economic revival in impoverished neighborhoods where federal dollars are increasingly insufficient to address the extreme needs of local residents. Also, they can operate independently from racist structures to accomplish their goals, and they can shape a theology that is not derived from slaveholding religion or beholden to denominational systems with mixed motives or conflicting needs. Yet this independence has a downside: megachurches often do not engage with other churches, black or white, in constructive ways to combat racism and to build bridges between different communities. Clearly, there is much to be learned from the ways black megachurches revitalize their neighborhoods and provide material hope to people who would otherwise be lost in the system, but better avenues of connection need to be built so that those lessons may be taught.

> *Black megachurches are able to help spark economic revival in impoverished neighborhoods where federal dollars increasingly are scarce or insufficient to address the extreme needs of local residents.*

Mainline Denominational Churches

Mainline denominational congregations, the most familiar and public form in this typology of African American churches, generally range in size from a few hundred to a few thousand worshipers. They are generally pastored by ministers who have had a substantial education, having completed not only college but also having gone through seminary. Pastors of these congregations are looked to as key leaders in the African American community, and politicians vie for the opportunity to appear in the pulpits of their churches just prior to election time. Some of these churches are connected with mainline Protestant denominations that are mostly white, such as the United Methodist Church, the American Baptist Churches, or Southern Baptist Convention, but the majority are from all-black denominations, such as the African Methodist Episcopal Church (AME), Church of God in Christ (COGIC), National Baptist Convention (NBC), and others.

Worship services in mainline black denominational churches are marked by great formal dignity, while at the same time they maintain the traits of enthusiastic worship that could be called black folk religion. They generally have outstanding choirs with effective organ accompaniment. The ministers often wear robes during worship services and will always be dressed with a certain degree of formality when out in public. In the same way, worship attendees always come dressed in their finest and most dignified apparel. White people who are used to "dressing down" for church often feel they are underdressed when they are guests in these black congregations.

Tony recalls a group of young white people who were on a work team in the neighborhood of his black church community. These young people attempted to come in for morning worship wearing jeans and t-shirts and found themselves barred at the door by the deacons. They were used to coming to church in this sort of informal attire, but the deacons told them that they couldn't come into the worship service dressed that way. The youth leader, who was in charge of this group of white teenagers became increasingly indignant and asked, "What kind of church is this that you have to be dressed like rich people to worship here? Is there no place for poor people in your church? Do you kick poor people out because they cannot afford the fine clothes like you're wearing?"

Casual dressing, characteristic among young people in white suburban churches these days (not to mention increasing numbers of middle-aged adults!), is not acceptable in mainline black congregations.

The deacon responded with some degree of anger and he said, "If the clothes you're wearing are the best clothes that you own, you would be welcome here. We don't shut anybody out because they're poor and don't have decent clothes to wear, but we do shut people out who do not bring into the church the best that they have. If you were going to see the president of the United States or the queen of England, would you go to visit them dressed like that? Or, would you put on your best suit with a shirt and tie? And would the girls be wearing proper dresses? Well, when you come into this church you're coming into the presence of the King of Kings and the Lord of Lords. When you come before such an awesome God you should wear the best clothes that you've got and offer him the best that you have. The way you're dressed is disrespecting our Lord, and we just won't let that happen here."

No doubt there is much truth in what the deacon had to say to those young people. Casual dressing, characteristic among young people in white suburban churches these days (not to mention increasing numbers of middle-aged adults!), and especially in white megachurches, is not acceptable in mainline black congregations. The pastor even said, "The church is the bride of Christ and when you come to the groom who is our Lord and Savior Jesus Christ you should come properly adorned."

The black church that Tony attends has in its membership several key political leaders of the city, including members of the city council, school board, and a U.S. congressman from the district of Philadelphia. Many prominent upper-middle-class professionals, including numerous doctors and lawyers, are common in the membership of the congregation, not to mention hosts of teachers. This sort of sophisticated membership is typical of many large mainline denominational black churches.

A sophisticated theology that matches this membership marks the sermons in Tony's church. The content of the sermons would gain approval among the theologically erudite; however, they are delivered in such a way that they tap into modes of expressions that have their roots in black ecclesiastical culture. There is an emotional quality in the spontaneity of the sermons that lifts verbal responses from those in the pews. When the pastor makes strong points, people throughout the congregation can be heard to shout out phrases like "Keep going!" or "That's right!" or "Okay now!" Tony, who has graduate degrees in theology, contends that his preacher has given some of the most profound and theologically sound sermons he has ever heard; yet he always employs a style that relates well to the black church tradition and the hundreds of people who worship in the congregation on Sunday morning.

The theologies and political value systems of black congregations of mainline denominations make them distinct from white Evangelical congregations in the same socioeconomic bracket (as noted in the previous chapter). Politically, black congregations still identify with the Democratic Party. Following the 2004 election, many political observers indentified "evangelicals" as a political block of the Republican Party, a base that provided overwhelming support for George W. Bush. This caused many black church leaders to shake their heads, saying that many overlook black Evangelical Christians and their politics. In reality, black congregations tend to be very evangelical in their theology. For example, they take their Bible very seriously and usually hold positions of scriptural inerrancy. Most black Christians accept without question the doctrines that underlie the Apostles' Creed. And, arguably, black churches contend that having a personal relationship with Jesus Christ as Lord and Savior is the only way to salvation more often than do white evangelical churches. In other words, black Christians tend, if anything, to be *more evangelical* than their white counterparts, but they do not identify with the political allegiances that have become characteristic of white Evangelicals.

> *Black Christians tend, if anything, to be more evangelical than their white counterparts for the most part; nevertheless, they do not identify with the political allegiances that have become characteristic of white evangelicals.*

African American Christians and Homosexuality

In the 2004 election, black Christians stayed mostly loyal to the Democratic Party largely because Republicans didn't support affirmative action programs that have significantly benefited black people across America. Yet, in spite of the overwhelming support that African American Christians gave to the Kerry/Edwards ticket, for the first time there was evidence of significant weakening of the allegiance that black Christians have had with Democrats. According to some analysts, this is primarily due the Democratic party's increasingly "gay friendly" platform and the African American community's overall high level of homophobia. When the issue of gay marriage emerged as a defining issue in the 2004 election, many prominent black preachers spoke out against the support that Democrats had given to gays and lesbians and, in some instances, urged their people to vote against any candidate who had a pro-gay stance.

In a dialogue on a Sunday morning news talk show during the 2004 election season, Tony spoke with one of the leading black ministers in America, who made it clear that his black membership voted with little enthusiasm for John Kerry. Unlike Jimmy Carter and Bill Clinton, they felt that Kerry lacked the ability to connect with African American people. This minister added that the liberal attitude that Democrats had on the "gay issue" had really turned off a lot of members of his congregation as well, despite the fact that Kerry and most other Democrats had not voiced support for gay marriage, only their opposition to President Bush's proposed constitutional amendment to ban such unions. (In the end blacks nationwide supported Kerry 89 percent, a drop of only 1 percent from their 2000 votes.)

The prejudices that many African American Christians have toward gay and lesbian people are difficult to understand in light of the positions taken by historic and prominent African American leaders on the "gay issue." For example, the Reverend Jesse Jackson, leader of the Rainbow Coalition and former presidential candidate, is a strong advocate for gay rights and supports gay marriage. The Reverend Al Sharpton, another 2004 candidate for the Democratic presidential nomination, also spoke out strongly in favor of gay rights, including support for the concept of gay marriage. Coretta Scott King, the widow of Martin Luther King Jr., has boldly stated, "If my husband were alive today, he would be a champion for gay and lesbian rights because my husband believed that when one group of people are oppressed within a society, everyone else in that society is also oppressed. Unless everyone is free, nobody is completely free."

On the other hand, many sociologists are not surprised by the reaction of African American Christians against gay and lesbian people and those who advocate equal rights and gay marriage. Sociologists believe that, in general, when an oppressed group gains acceptance within a given society, that group has a tendency to seek out some other group to take its role as an oppressed minority. In playing that "we-they" game, the group seeking social acceptance believes that it gains status by defining itself as the "we" that makes up the dominant group in the society and defining a new out-group to take its place as the object of prejudice and discrimination. The group that gains new acceptance has a strong tendency to affirm the hierarchical form of membership of the dominant social group and joins it by putting down the new group of people who are declared unacceptable. As of late, that new group is the gay and lesbian community.

Issues of gentrification may also be aggravating this antagonism against the gay and lesbian community, even among those who call themselves Christians. For instance, in one historically black neighborhood in Washington, D.C., whose beautiful Victorian mansions and brick townhouses had fallen into disrepair and the streets overrun with drugs and prostitution, many gay men started buying up the properties and restoring them to their original splendor. This development brought sharp criticism from a prominent African American Baptist pastor when members of his congregation ran into a dispute with their new white, gay neighbors over Sunday morning parking arrangements. He accused these gentrifiers not only of being racist but also of being anti-church on account of their homosexuality. This brought countercharges of homophobia from the gays (particularly when the pastor referred to lesbians as "dykes" when visiting a neighboring church's pulpit). Eventually, the church decided to move to a new development in the suburbs, but the wounds from the dispute remain among those black and white people of all sexual orientations who are learning to share and revitalize the neighborhood together.

We find it disheartening to hear some current leaders in the African American community making public statements in which they have declared loud and clear that they do not deem gay people to deserve being part of the Civil Rights movement. Gay rights, they claim, have nothing to do with civil rights. Thus, the group that once was denied its rights is now all too ready to turn around and deny rights to a new group seeking justice and equality within the American social system. What these black church people fail to realize is that by opposing gay rights they are forming alliances with the same people who are responsible for discriminating against them only a few years ago and who still maintain prejudices and racist values that reinforce unjust structures within American society.

Connecting Black Churches and White Churches

In all three incarnations of the black church, there are important points at which white churches can connect with them for the benefit of the community and Christiantiy itself. Yet when white churches endeavor to establish some kind of connection with the African American community, they usually reach out only to the black mainline denominational churches; storefronts and megachurches are often left out of ecumenical and interracial partnerships. Regardless of who is invited to the table, however, it is good when any church tries to plan programs in which white and black communities can come together and share in a unified way to serve their communities. Usually, however, these combined efforts of black and white churches supposedly working together are organized around special preaching services, usually of an evangelistic nature. But when the nights of these special services arrive, the black congregations often fail to show up.

When white pastors are asked about this phenomenon in private, they often comment that black pastors regard their local churches as private kingdoms. "Everything is evaluated on whether or not interracial programs enhance the growth and prosperity of their [black pastors'] respective congregations," one white pastor told Tony. Another white pastor told him, in reference to a particular black minister, "All he's interested in is his little kingdom. If we can deliver resources and support for what he's trying to do in his own church, he's more than willing to cooperate. But if it is not something that will deliver immediate benefits to his own congregation, he will pretend to be cooperative but in the end will not move his people to any unified effort with us and the larger community."

The role of the black pastor in his or her church undoubtedly carries with it a great deal of status. It has been said that in the black community the pastor is the king of the congregation; decision-making power usually resides almost completely in his or her hands. So there is some degree of truth in what the white pastor had to say.

On the other hand, white churches seldom have a realistic view of how racial integration takes place across church lines. White pastors often think they have done all that is necessary when they verbally state that their churches are nondiscriminatory and that black people are welcome in their congregations. What they don't realize is that the black people who join these white churches often would be in the upper socioeconomic brackets of black congregations. In short, white churches, especially in the suburbs, are all too ready to welcome black professionals into their membership, but not the lower classes. White churches will even take a certain degree of pride in pointing out that they have black people who are in their pews without recognizing that any congregation would be thrilled to have doctors, lawyers, teachers, and other professionals in their churches, regardless of racial identity. These white churches open their doors to well-to-do African American congregants and seldom receive those who come from the underclass of the social system. Seldom do those on public welfare or with prison records show up in these mainline, upper-middle-class, white churches.

Because of this unconscious problem among white churches, it is little wonder that black pastors are reluctant to introduce their members to white pastors and white congregations and to encourage racial integration. To the black pastor, such integration usually means the loss of their brightest, most successful members to white churches—while their black congregations get nothing in return (that is, rarely do upper-class whites join black churches). What often happens in black churches is that some of their best financial contributors end up supporting white churches instead of the black churches where they came from. In short, racial integration can actually work to the detriment of black pastors and their churches by facilitating the loss of some of the key people who have been part of their community.

The best way for racial integration to take place in our churches is for white Christians from middle- and upper-class congregations to attend black church worship services and eventually become members of those churches. They will find that black congregations will be more than happy to receive them; indeed, white people who join black churches have generally been warmly received. They have been embraced by black pastors of those churches and are treated as special people. If white pastors really want to facilitate racial integration, they should consider commissioning some of their key contributing members to join black inner-city churches, taking their talents and their resources to those new church affiliations. White pastors inviting talented and affluent blacks to attend their congregations is not going to help racial integration as much as sending some of the most talented and financially viable members of white churches to be a part of black congregations that often need their resources and skills.

> *The best way for racial integration to take place in our churches is for white Christians from those middle- and upper-class congregations to attend black church worship services and eventually become members of those churches.*

Clearly, there are many productive ways that black and white churches can work together to build racial understanding and to rectify inequities that beset the black community. In Part Two, we will look at some of the theological and spiritual resources that reside not only in the American church but also in the experience and beliefs of black Christians in Africa, and explore further avenues for promoting racial reconciliation.

Part Two

A RECONCILING
CHURCH

CHAPTER 7

A Community of Hope

Insights from Africa point the way beyond individualism and racism to true Christian community.

In looking at the racist history and culture of American Evangelicalism, we showed how a theology grounded in individualism not only anchors that faith tradition but also influences how white Evangelicals engage the political sphere, and thus the human community, in general. In fact, individualism pervades Western culture and most forms of Christianity. We wish to counter this rabid individualism by describing Western and African views of spirituality that emphasize what we all have in common. In these worldviews, we discover common sight through our particular cultures, we gain a common hope, and we open up a balanced vision of God in our midst.

The ultimate, or eschatological, hope we present here is one in which there will be community enough for all persons to discover their destiny together. It is often only through either direct cross-cultural experience or vicariously through study of other cultures that one begins to imagine in intelligible ways how those who are different may find a common destiny. First, we find this vision by comparing Western and African epistemology (ways of knowing), which allows us to think more clearly about the goal, or end, of the spiritual life. Second, we claim that African sensibilities inhabit what we call "sacramental balance." The primary aim of such balance is to facilitate the full journey of individuals and communities to their complete goal in the life of God. In the same way, sensitivity to the difference of worldviews relating to the spiritual life is thus a prerequisite for fruitful, grace-filled sharing and discernment of the fullness of our ultimate destination. We conclude that African eschatological vision provides a needed corrective to the near-sighted vision of Western religious persons.

Western and African Ways of Knowing

Even in the church we find the frightening world of survival-of-the-fittest culture, a jockeying for power and prestige. If we in the church still have a problem of coming into the kingdom of heaven, of allowing God to pull us into the kingdom of God, then this eschatological process of becoming persons must be understood as an ongoing process, one that takes all of our life to sort out.

In the West, especially from the time of the Enlightenment, the self has been understood as a distinct individual, with unique value and distinct rights. Such personal emphasis places supreme value on the right of self-determination, self-achievement, and self-satisfaction. It is often justified by claiming that such personal responsibility for the shaping of one's life is a good and flows from the traditional Judeo-Christian understanding of the dignity and worth of each human being. But one of the major weaknesses in this personal-dimension worldview is the lack of criteria for how a person bonds with his or her community. This lack of criteria, especially in modernity and particularly in North American culture, accentuates personal salvation as the primary lens for understanding Christian spirituality. This Western notion of spirituality has profoundly influenced all facets of life, including politics, economics, and religion (as we have already explored in reference to Evangelicalism). More important, this Western criterion of spirituality is informed by an eschatology (our notions of ultimate purpose

> *It is often only through either direct cross-cultural experience or vicariously through study of other cultures that one begins to imagine in intelligible ways how those who are different may find a common destiny.*

and destiny) in which personal salvation becomes the normative goal of life. We learn from African Christian spirituality, however, that eschatology must always be balanced between personal and community salvation.

According to African sensibilities, the totally self-sufficient human being is subhuman. We depend on others to learn how to be human, how to think as a human being, how to eat as a human being, how to walk as a human being. That is why the cutthroat competitiveness of the so-called free enterprise system is so disturbing for African persons such as former South African Archbishop Desmond Tutu.[1] We should not have to compete against other people to know ourselves; rather, our self-knowledge should proceed from our cooperation with one another. Archbishop Tutu explains this problem through a particular example of how Western culture tends to depend on competition to form human identity:

> One day at a party in England for some reason we were expected for our tea. I offered to buy a cup for an acquaintance. Now, he could have said: "No, thank you." You could have knocked me down with a feather when he replied, "No, I won't be subsidized!" Well, I never. I suppose it was an understandable attitude. You want to pay your own way and not sponge on others. But it is an attitude that many have seemed to carry over into our relationship with God—our refusal to be subsidized by God. It all stems very much from the prevailing achievement ethic which permeates our very existence. It is drummed into our heads from our most impressionable days that you must succeed. At school you must not just do well, no, you must grind the opposition into the dust. We get so worked up that our children can become nervous wrecks as they are egged on to greater efforts by competitive parents. Our culture has it that ulcers have become status symbols.[2]

A system that encourages a high degree of competitiveness and selfishness in a world that seems to have been made for interdependence must have something seriously wrong with it. Something is clearly amiss in a system of people whose goal is to achieve success despite the resulting dehumanization. To put it more provocatively, competition is the sign of the fall of creation. It is the opposite of *Ubuntu*, an African term that connotes the basic connectedness of all human beings beyond all lines of race and class. Tutu describes that interconnectedness in a playful manner:

> Have you seen a symphony orchestra? They are all dolled and beautiful with their magnificent instruments, cellos, violins, etc. Sometimes dolled up as the rest, is a chap at the back carrying a triangle. Now and again the conductor will point to him and he will play "ting." That might seem so insignificant but in the conception of the composer something irreplaceable would be lost to the total beauty of the symphony if that "ting" did not happen.[3]

When a Western person, formed in a worldview of the sole importance of the individual, meets an African person, the Western person meets someone whose experience of the self is distinctly different from the Western eschatology of personal salvation. In contrast to the West, the African individual does not exist apart from the community. The African person is part of the whole, and African identity flows from the community experience and never in isolation from it, especially since it is African community that defines who an African person is and who an African person becomes. This is not a utilitarian sensibility, such as many Westerners want to impose on African community. Instead, in African eschatology, the uniqueness of each person is affirmed and acknowledged, but African individuality and freedom are always balanced

When a Western person, formed in a worldview of the sole importance of the individual, meets an African person, the Western person meets someone whose experience of the self is distinctly different from the Western eschatology of personal salvation.

by the destiny of the community. From this balanced destiny we conclude that African eschatology is more concerned about communal salvation than the personal salvation so often envisioned by Western Christian spirituality. We can learn from that.

Sacramentality as Eschatological Balance

For the African person, all of life is one continuous movement of community from birth to death and beyond. An African person acts therefore in concert with the community and not apart from it in order to find salvation in God. Crucial to an African spirituality of community is the idea that the destiny of the individual and the community are bound together in experiencing ultimate salvation. The classic phrasing of this intrinsic relationship was first stated by African theologian John Mbiti and carried on by Desmond Tutu, as an *Ubuntu* sensibility, namely, "I am, because we are; and since we are, therefore I am."[4] When good is envisioned, it is good for the entire community; and when evil is committed, the shame or the victimization affects the whole community. Therefore, inherent to African eschatology is the understanding that all persons are vitally and organically bonded in community in such a way that this union extends to the salvation of all of creation.

An African person discovers his or her self by learning what is expected of each person in relationship to a clan. That is where cultural norms and responsibilities become intelligible. An African person balances the destiny of the community and individual through the various initiation rites that have been and, to a certain extent, still remain vital to the interpretation of what is African. The rites of passage practiced among African communities have a sacramental character and integrate the person into the society so that she or he may find identity within community. Appropriate to the understanding of African eschatology, these rites of passage continue beyond death, since ancestors are regarded as continuing parts of the community, able to influence events and to guide the community toward maturity. This emphasis upon maturity and passage into deeper stages flows from an African eschatological sense of personhood in which the individual becomes conscious of her- or himself through the ultimate vision of social interaction with God and neighbor.

Interpreted through Christian faith, this ultimate vision manifests into the communion of saints. Therefore, an African person discovers criteria for sainthood through the ongoing relationship between those who still live on Earth and those who have died and moved into a deeper state of being. Those who move most deeply into the spiritual life become known as elders and ultimately as ancestors in African traditions. *In essence, African personhood is understood through rites of passage toward an eschatological end.* Through these initiation rites, all of life is seen as sacramental, as visible signs of invisible grace.

> *In contrast to Western spirituality, the African goal of asceticism is not to be alone; on the contrary, the African person strives to match daily reality with the ultimate vision of the communion of saints.*

Traditionally, in Western Christian spirituality, such saintly pursuit is described as asceticism. Interestingly enough, Christian asceticism was defined first in Africa by St. Antony, who is best known as the progenitor of the desert tradition in which many practiced their eschatological visions in a daily routine. Among African sensibilities, self-denial in community is not done to achieve personal salvation; rather, African Christian spirituality envisions that nature in all its dimensions is alive with God's presence, and therefore one will need to practice asceticism to be made more available to the presence of God and community. In contrast to Western spirituality, the African goal of asceticism is not to be alone; on the contrary, the African person strives to match daily reality with the ultimate vision of the communion of saints.[5]

Although Western influences of various kinds profoundly affect African society, this African experience of the self in community remains the foundation of African self-understanding.

It is clear, then, what misunderstandings can easily occur in this pursuit of defining African spirituality in the Western world. When Western persons urge African persons to assume both a degree of self-consciousness and self-assertion, the African person's cultural and spiritual experience is such that Western preoccupation with self-contained, personal spirituality does not translate well into recognizable African sensibilities. This leads to an interesting problem for traditional Western Christian spirituality in which the individual, through asceticism and spiritual disciplines, becomes responsible for his or her own spiritual growth.

Creating Community through Creation

In the same way that an African person is vitally and organically bonded in community with others, this union is extended to the pursuits of being one with God and all of creation. Consider the desert tradition mentioned above, through which we learn that the African practices of asceticism share with the Judeo-Christian tradition the idea that the end, or *telos*, of humanity is found in God as Creator of the material universe.[6] The ultimate goal in African Christian spirituality is to live with God, who people experience through creation. How African persons practice God's presence through creation is very difficult for Western minds to comprehend outside of negative descriptions, portraying African spirituality as superstition or idolatry. But far from such negative and simplistic understandings of African sacramentality, African practices of the divine in creation are profound. For example, different groups, such as the Ashanti of Ghana, speak of various "small gods" (*abosom*) or minor divinities that are associated with natural phenomena such as lakes, rivers, trees, and so on. African theologian John Pobee points out that "the gods are not the stone or tree or river itself, but that they may from time to time be contacted at a concrete habitation, though they are not confined therein."[7] In other words, in African spirituality, all of creation is charged with the presence of the invisible—God and the spirit world, both good and evil—and so it is said that "African peoples 'see' that invisible universe when they look at, hear or feel the visible and tangible world."[8] This is what we mean by African sacramentality.

African sacramentality sees a universe alive with power that generates both fear and awe. Most characteristic of African sacramentality is the desire to live in harmony with nature, not apart from it. John Mbiti states that African "people report that they see the spirits in ponds, caves, groves, mountains or outside their villages, dancing, singing, herding cattle, working in their fields or nursing their children."[9] In African sacramentality, one understands that the spirits can communicate with persons through dreams, visions, and mediums. The relationships of spirits vary with each African society, but the sense of the presence of the spirit is pervasive for both Christians and African traditional believers.

The Sacred and Profane in African Spirituality

This understanding of pervasive spirit leads us into a needed discussion of the sacred and the profane in African spirituality. The origin of African spirits, both sacred and profane, affects African community. An understanding of this African pneumatology (idea of spirit) is important to distinguishing between African Christian spirituality and African spirituality. The former is linked to the community of the saints, while the latter is linked to the ancestors. Both, however, engage the dynamic of sacred and profane spirit. A person is or is not accepted into the community of ancestors based on how she or he lived in community in this earthly life.

These communal and sacramental elements of the African view of the world and creation are distinctly different in many ways from the Western perspective. The African person's understanding of spirituality offers to us Western persons a sense of sacred relationship and the experience of harmony with nature, a nondomineering attitude toward nature, a sense of the invisible world alive in the visible, and a strong conviction that various spirits can communicate with persons and the community. These African understandings challenge Western perceptions of the profane character of the universe, a sense of control over it, and typical skepticism about the existence of any kinds of spirits or similar beings with power to influence human behavior. Within this complexity we are then led to the African understandings of *Ubuntu,* which illustrates how African individuality and freedom are always balanced by the destiny of the community.

During the past several hundred years religious belief, practice, and experience have become optional for Western persons and not a core way to organize life experience. Even for those who remain believers, too often religion becomes a separate compartment of life, with various religious duties to be "done" but with little influence on ordinary life other than the vague desire to do good and respect the rights of others. One attends church on Sunday and then gives little thought to religious commitment the rest of the week.

> *The African person's understanding of spirituality offers to us Western persons a sense of sacred relationship and the experience of harmony with nature, a nondomineering attitude toward nature, a sense of the invisible world alive in the visible, and a strong conviction that various spirits can communicate with persons and the community.*

Organized religion in the West has seen its influence decline in many ways as the dichotomy between religious and secular has become more pronounced. Even the rise of various fundamentalist groups has not challenged this trajectory much because personal faith is seen as operative in a fairly narrow, restricted sphere with little social or political implication for the wider society. The Western person brings much of this perspective to spirituality when the matter to be discussed is only that which is "religious." Prayer experience is important, but one's involvement with a local political party is not. Any approach or suggestion that reinforces this dichotomy in Western experience between "religion" and "life" widens the gap.

African experience is radically different, as we have seen, for religion is seen as inseparable from African culture. In African traditional religions, formal distinctions between the sacred and the secular, the spiritual and the material dimensions of life, do not exist. Life and religious expression are one, since the invisible world of the sacred is so intimately linked with ordinary life. The universe is basically a religious universe. African spirituality is thus a daily affair, permeating every aspect of life: rising; getting water; cooking food; going to the farm, office, or school; attending a funeral or wedding; drinking beer with friends. Certain religious rituals surround specific life events such as birth and death, but the African spiritual worldview is broader, encompassing all that is human and part of life. The African who becomes a Christian or Muslim or follower of any other world religion looks for an experience of spirituality that encompasses his or her whole life: language, thought patterns, social relationships, attitudes, values, desires, fears. It is not enough to "do religious things" regularly, since the African's desire is for a spiritual worldview that will fill the world with meaning and be especially sustaining in times of fear and crisis.

> *African spirituality is a daily affair, permeating every aspect of life: rising; getting water; cooking food; going to the farm, office, or school; attending a funeral or wedding; drinking beer with friends.*

African Christian spirituality offers a cosmology not just for the continent of Africa but for the whole world to participate in gaining spiritual sight for how we all relate to each other and to creation. In African Christian spirituality, the African person brings her or his desire to find the experience of God in every facet of life without exception. Western Christians, formed in the pattern of religion as one part of life, can be disconcerted by the wholistic view presented by their African brothers or sisters, but we have much to gain from African Christian spirituality. At the same time, the distinct values of both African and Western worldviews can enrich each other, with the Western person learning the value of communal experience as formative of the self, and the African person coming to a deeper awareness of individual uniqueness. In the next chapter, we will explore how this African understanding can inform efforts toward racial reconciliation between white and black churches in the United States.

CHAPTER 8

A Commitment to Justice

Reconciliation flows from spiritual commitment.
It entails the hard work of restorative justice.

African understandings of *Ubuntu*—the interconnectedness of the individual and community—lead us naturally to reflect on how such a perspective can fuel Christian efforts toward racial reconciliation. Reconciliation is the slow, arduous work of Christians. In our Christian baptisms, we claim to embody the continuing presence and memory of Christ in the world. This work of being a Christian is not a quick fix, as the past two millennia clearly demonstrate, but rather the deliberate engagement that often involves discomfort and unease.

In the face of such a challenge, it is helpful to recall Paul's reminder that we are a new creation: "From now on, therefore, we regard [remember] no one from a human point of view [or, according to the flesh]" (2 Cor. 5:16). To live according to the flesh simply means to follow the instinctual human urge toward destruction of self and community. "So if anyone is in Christ, there is a new creation: everything old has passed away; see, everything has become new! All this is from God, who reconciled us to himself through Christ, and has given us the ministry of reconciliation" (2 Cor. 5:17-18). The paradox in all of this is that Paul is asking the Corinthian community to "remember" that all things have passed away; in other words, to remember a new reality. Paul is asking the Corinthian community not just to get the words right about life in Christ but also to *embody* the memory of Christ in the difficult circumstances of being a Christian in Corinth. It is impossible for us as human beings to retain anything as a pure memory; instead, we must *embody* memory. And the way that Paul teaches not only Christians of his time and context but us as well is through his conclusion, "All this is from God, who reconciled us to himself through Christ, and has given us the ministry of reconciliation." Paul helps us see that the embodiment of Christ's memory is practiced through the ministry of reconciliation. How can we think through the embodiment or practice of a ministry of reconciliation today?

Desmond Tutu and the Ministry of Reconciliation

Perhaps the most profound illustration of such a ministry of reconciliation in recent memory is the experience of South Africa's efforts toward reconciliation following the collapse of apartheid. For two years (1993 and 1994) Michael lived in South Africa and it was during that turbulent time, living in a nation-state that had finally decided to practice democracy, that he discovered an exemplar of this ministry of reconciliation—the life and thought of Archbishop Tutu. The context of South African apartheid presented the dilemma in which Tutu, as ecclesial head of a historically white church, negotiated how to act effectively in a society so defined by race that both Afrikaner and African could each claim God's election as chosen. Subsequently, he served as head of South Africa's Truth and Reconciliation Commission, where his work toward restorative justice cannot be reduced simply to an effort to restore black people to a place of flourishing—such an interpretation forfeits his profound contributions to *reconciliation* of peoples, which lie in his pastoral theology.

Tutu's pastoral theology operates from a distinctively spiritual model of forgiveness in which human identity is modeled on a trinitarian image of God, namely, the flourishing relation of diverse persons in unity. This trinitarian spirituality generates a pastoral theology of community in which all people—black, white, Xhosa, Afrikaner, gay and lesbian, women and men—have an opportunity to grow toward unity. Moreover, this understanding of personhood assumes that there is no such thing as a reprobate. Indeed, as a pastor, Tutu is trained to be sensitive to even a flickering ember of remorse in the hope that it could be nurtured into a flame of reconciliation: "We all have the capacity to become saints."[1] Therefore, not to forgive assumes there is no such image of God among humanity. More specifically, not to forgive assumes no future for South Africa or any other society.[2]

Yet Tutu believes not only in forgiveness but also in repentance. He practices both because his context—white justification of apartheid and black political liberation—is shaped by competing claims on God's election whereby one group is privileged over another. Instead of conceptualizing race as determining identity—and therefore the privilege of God's favor—Tutu adheres theologically to a metanarrative of God's forgiveness. In this metanarrative, conflicting racial identities are expressed and defined in the reconciling concept of *imago Dei*—the image of God—revealed through Jesus Christ who manifested both the abundance and fulfillment of relational personhood. Jesus points the way to reconciliation.

> *Tutu's pastoral theology operates from a distinctively theological model of forgiveness in which human identity is modeled on a trinitarian image of God, namely, the flourishing relation of diverse persons in unity.*

Christianity's most radical practice, informed by Jesus's story, is forgiveness. Jesus allows us to see that we need to be forgiven by someone greater than ourselves. This makes Christians conscious of a deep illness and need for a healer. The metanarrative of God's forgiveness entails an ongoing story of human illness described through our incessant violence and abuse against self and other. Jesus's radical narrative of forgiveness aims to discover the truth about the past so that there may be a future (hence the title of Tutu's book *No Future without Forgiveness*).

So Tutu's political contributions flow directly from his theology. Tutu understands that true political confession is spiritual, the act of reconciling memory embodied by the only One qualified to judge whether the truth has been told and forgiveness merited, God in Jesus Christ. Tutu's embodiment of memory, therefore, derives from Jesus's discipleship. His pastoral approach to justice seeks healing from apartheid, which divides and conquers like malignant cells. Such a disease demonstrates the greatest deviation from a triune God's creation of interdependence. It is essential that we see the connection between the disease of apartheid in need of pastoral care and the disease of individualism in the West in need of pastoral care. Tutu says:

> Disease disconnects the sufferer from the body and the person she or he has been, and it disconnects the sufferer from the network of relationships that has made it valuable to be that person. The ways our society treats the ill—the transformation of identity from person to patient—creates further disconnections. The person whom others have interacted with reciprocally as "you" becomes "he" who must be taken care of.[3]

Unlike such individualistic medicine, our healing enables us to find our deepest self in Christ. Regarded through this sort of theological lens, it then follows that the Christian must concede to the need to be transformed into a new identity, as Paul exhorted. This new perspective fully encompasses the truth that Tutu states: "God does not love us because we are lovable, but we are lovable precisely because God loves us. God's love is what gives us our worth. . . . So we are liberated from the desire to achieve, to impress. We are the children of the divine love and nothing can change that fundamental fact about us."[4] In the same way, this profoundly Christian statement appeals to the ancient African concepts of the harmony between individual and community we have identified as *Ubuntu*.

The beatitude of *Ubuntu* is that it provides an alternative to vengeance and an invaluable perspective in which white and black people may see themselves as more than racial rivals. "When you look at someone with eyes of love," Tutu believes, "you see a reality differently from that of someone who looks at the same person without love, with hatred or even just indifference."[5] That lack of love, that hatred or indifference, is how racism forms persons, how it legitimates evil structures that masquerade as the common good.

Tutu believes that *Ubuntu* shows us how personhood forms ultimately through the church, which witnesses to the world that God loves human identities into being—that an individuals' identities are established before they can even conceive of justice or tyranny. In other words, God's love is prevenient—it is there before everything else and calls all justifications for control into account. For Christians, no one can claim control of life. A true vision of how to be in the world is grounded in the life of grace in God. Any claim of control or power is a delusion—we are all vulnerable. And indeed, *Ubuntu* denotes an environment of vulnerability, that is, a set of relationships in which persons are able to recognize that their humanity is bound up in the other's humanity. When one lives in *Ubuntu,* instead of being manipulative and self-seeking one is "more willing to make excuses for others"[6] and even discover new meaning in other persons—an attribute that distinguishes humans from other animals.

Through an embodiment of spiritual memory that is not quietistic, passive, or individualistic, Tutu's pastoral care proactively reverses the devisive pattern of apartheid. *Ubuntu* seeks a paradigm in which the affliction of African people can be transfigured through forgivenes, and race is a much less significant category of identity. Instead of retaliation and further competition among Christian narratives of privilege, African people are to turn toward God and see that their God also was afflicted. Instead of killing each other because they are black or white, they are to rejoice in how God has created persons differently so that new meanings and identities are always possible. Even if African people seem hopelessly trapped in the closed system of apartheid and racial classifications, the image of God is planted in human beings in such a way that, like plants slowly responding to light, we will one day manifest the kingdom of God. Grace, like light, percolates through creation.

Perspective determines actions. *Ubuntu* provides an invaluable perspective in which white and black people may see themselves as more than racial rivals. Just as the vision of *Ubuntu* is transforming South Africa, so can this vision transform the many divisions that traumatize American society and churches today. Reconciliation is one: You cannot separate justice from the Judeo-Christian understanding of *shalom* for all creation. Resolutions for the tensions of our day—between right and left, rich and poor, those of color and those called white, women and men, homosexual and heterosexual—cannot simply come from a consensus of ideas, for such a consensus will never occur. Rather, we must look to spiritual practices focused on the acknowledgment and flourishing of diverse peoples who have learned to be more than warring parties. Our practice of reconciliation repairs our common life and thoughts. Restorative justice is one such process that has the potential to transform us.

> *The beatitude of Ubuntu is that it provides an alternative to vengeance and an invaluable perspective in which white and black people may see themselves as more than racial rivals.*

Restorative Justice

In South Africa, reconciliation has taken place through restorative justice processes overseen by the Truth and Reconciliation Commission (TRC), headed by Archbishop Tutu. Such programs have been adopted not only in other countries seeking recovery from a history of oppression and violence, but in criminal justice systems, schools, and other systems worldwide where there is need for healing that steers away from the model of vengeful retributive justice, our normal system, tends to embrace. In retributive justice, the offender is held accountable according to criteria that match the crime with the appropriate punishment. According to this philosophy, a crime

deserves a matching punishment, and even a deterrent to prevent
such a crime to occur again.

By contrast, we regard restorative justice as offering consider-
able potential for changing the way in which society puts right the
harm caused by racism and violence. Therefore, it needs a corre-
sponding restorative theology. Our task is to explore ways in which
Christians practice restorative theology
as a path to dealing with violence—
and indeed, racism is a form of violence—which seeks to corrupt human
identity. Jesus has already determined
that the goal of human identity is to
become mutual with God. Restorative
theology is hard, however, for us to
commit to because of how we respond to those who do us harm,
especially to those we call criminals. It seeks to heal the separation
caused by harm done by a perpetrator not only to a victim but also
to society.

> *Restorative theology, as it
> follows the examples of Jesus's
> life, death, resurrection, and
> ascension, allows a better
> vision for humanity, justice,
> healing, and restoration.*

Yet restorative theology, as it follows the examples of Jesus's
life, death, resurrection, and ascension, must be taken seriously
because it allows a better vision for *humanity, justice, healing, and
restoration.* Just as Tutu announced that "we all have the capacity to become saints," so in restorative theology, neither victim
nor perpetrator is fixed in their identities. Instead, both need correction and restoration to their full *humanity.* The story of Jesus
allows us to believe not only that this is possible, but that it is a
better, deeper way of *justice* than that of retribution. By adhering
to the story of Jesus, which is a narrative of forgiveness, *healing*
takes place so that victims can release their anger and offenders can relinquish violence. Offenders are thereby enabled to be
restored to society as useful contributing members, and victims
are restored to new productivity as well—such *restoration* changes
them beyond their previous identities in which retributive justice
would leave them fixed.

Offenders are changed because instead of the idea of whatever
prompted their offense, they are able to see a person (a key factor

for Desmond Tutu and the TRC). They are changed because they can reframe and newly understand their excuses and rationalizations (following the thinking of Simone Weil). They are changed because of the miracle of the victim's forgiveness and becoming accountable to a new identity (a principle espoused by Anglican Archbishop Rowan Williams). They are changed because they are no longer socially paralyzed—new incentive is given to imagine life with dignity (thus invoking the liberation theology of James Cone). They participate in a new kind of power in which the goal becomes relief from all that burdens our souls (informed by Catholic spiritual writer Michael Crosby).

Restorative justice works from the following principles, as identified by expert Marian Liebmann:

- Victim support and healing is a priority
- Offenders take responsibility for what they have done
- There is dialogue to achieve understanding
- There is an attempt to put right the harm done
- Offenders look at how to avoid future offending
- The community helps to reintegrate both victims and offenders
- It acknowledges the wrong that has been done to victims
- It holds offenders accountable for what they have done
- It provides offenders with an opportunity to make reparation to victims
- It provides victims with an opportunity to receive reparation for the harm done
- It allows both victims and offenders to move on
- It enables society to become safer because it effectively reduces further violence[7]

How does all of this help us with the problem of racism? First, by offering mediation between victim and offender, persistent problems of racism are directly addressed and dealt with. By offering them the opportunity to communicate with each other, either directly or indirectly, they also gain the opportunity for greater understanding of self and of one another, and sometimes for reparation. When offenders understand and accept the harmful impact of their behavior, they are more likely not only to apologize or make reparations but also to change their behaviors. Sometimes, this mediation may involve what criminal expert John Braithwaite has called "reintegrative shaming" as a sanction for the unacceptable behavior.[8] Such shaming can be more effective than punishment if it is specifically aimed at restoring the offender to society and does not lead to meaningless stigma and rejection. (Indeed, this sort of shaming is different from that which surrounds modern racism, which tends to mire people in silence.)

Second, a specifically negotiated reparation provides the gravity for the harm done and demonstrates that the offender takes responsibility for her or his offense. The victim and the offender are thus linked by a relationship based on forgiveness, rather than a separation that seeks to maintain itself perpetually, with ever-escalating levels of punishment. (Again, this sort of reparation differs from recent political calls among some African Americans for slavery reparations, which are grounded neither in true forgiveness nor repentance.)

Third, in a retributive justice system, the criminal justice process tends to racialize crime, a stigmatization that spills over into church and society. Restorative theology helps both victims and prosecutors to resist such racialization, thus permitting offenders to move beyond the static existence of being called criminals. As conflict-resolution specialist Annette Hinton writes, "This is Justice that is relevant. It is also Justice that is healing."[9]

Restorative justice is very much in line with the nature of God shown through Scripture. The problem, however, for understanding justice as God's nature, is that we often lack full initiation into the ways of God. The argument of many against this approach to justice is that (1) some say they do not understand God the way we do; (2) some say we have God all wrong; and (3) some say human beings cannot participate in the nature of God. We assert that all Christians are invited to know the same God and to be initiated into the nature of God whose justice is not our kind of justice. Indeed, by participating in restorative justice processes, we also participate in the nature of God.

The Fruit of Restorative Justice

The results of restorative justice can be seen most profoundly in the work of the Truth and Reconciliation Commission, which some observers see as a cathartic process. Such a self-cleansing must lead to a turmoil of emotions—anger, sadness, grief, and shock—that must be allowed to surface. The emotions that rose in many black South African people conflict deeply with the typical Western European cultural disposition, which regards the past as over and finished. Although Europeans and Americans tend to honor their dead, they do not often live with the awareness that the spirits of the dead are still with them and that it is of vital importance to reconcile the unredeemed spirits of the past. This is, however, a conviction deeply rooted in black African spirituality. For Africans there can be no peaceful presence as long as the spirits of the dead are not laid to rest. Therefore, many relatives of murdered or disappeared persons ask the TRC to help them get back from the police whatever remains exist of their loved ones in order to bury them in a decent and dignified manner. The burial is the ritual by which a lost member of the family can finally be brought home. This is the way in which harmony between the generations is restored and maintained. Bringing home the one who is lost, even the one who is guilty, to the place of the ancestors is a vital aspect of the peace of the living.

As we saw in the prior chapter, this is a spirituality that should not be denounced as belief in "spirits" but as a worldview that knows something of the fundamental connectedness of all life. It is a spirituality that sees each individual human being as a member of the community, a community that includes the past and the coming generations. In this context, coming to terms with the past is more than settling legal claims; it is an act of re-membering, of bringing together what belongs together. African re-membering has a lot to do with healing, redemption, and liberation.

Concepts like *Ubuntu* help African peoples to transcend the violent mechanisms of denial and retaliation that are typical of Western cultures. For Tutu, forgiveness does not rest in itself; rather it assumes God's sovereignty, enticing all to repentance. This raised several questions: Would white people in South Africa be prepared to see the TRC as an opportunity to gain a deeper understanding of the spiritual power of their black fellow citizens? Would whites learn from blacks to work for processes of re-membering, of bringing peace to the past for the sake of the present and future? Would they grasp the great readiness of the victims to forgive them as a chance to leave the prisons of shame and the dungeons of denial so that all the people at the Cape of Good Hope can finally be of good hope?

> *Coming to terms with the past is more than settling legal claims; it is an act of re-membering, of bringing together that belongs together.*

As women and men, victims and witnesses recalled their memories, they were again faced with all their pain and anguish. And yet, as these persons faced their suffering, and as they named it in public, they left the witness stand with their heads held high. They were recognized in their pain, and this is the beginning of a renewed dignity. They were once destined to be annihilated, but now they are presented as heroes. When they were tortured in the prisons they were told, "Yell as loud as you wish, nobody will ever hear you!" but now the nation hears. The accounts of their suffering have been received into the memories of the nation. Once they were made voiceless, but now their voice can be heard across radio and television. Now the names of the torturers, who were beyond reproach only a few years ago, can be spoken openly. This correction of history is restorative for all who had been humiliated—victim and perpetrator—bringing to mind the Magnificat of Mary: "He has put down the mighty from their thrones, and exalted those of low degree" (Luke 1:52). This profound satisfaction is not a subliminal form of revenge. It expresses itself in genuine readiness to forgive. Many victims repeated the phrase expressed by a witness during the first days of the TRC hearings: "I am ready to forgive, but I need to know whom and for what."

Can we imagine what might happen if restorative justice processes, such as those that have been transforming South Africa, were brought to bear upon the long history of slavery and oppression in the United States? What if black and white churches came together to create the safe space within which African Americans could witness to the pain resulting from racism, and white Americans could confess and apologize for their complicity with racist structures? How might restorative justice processes transform the American criminal justice system, which incarcerates and executes young African American men at a rate that far exceeds that of their white peers? How must our theology and spirituality be transformed to create the environment in which reconciliation and restoration may flourish? Our closing chapters will seek answers to these questions.

CHAPTER 9

A Spirituality of Healing

If we are one in Christ, then through us his way of liberation and love can heal a suffering world.

The oppression of black people in both the United States and South Africa, the promise of restorative theology, and the concept of *Ubuntu* all point to the key themes that have shaped black theology and enable us to envision a healing spirituality grounded in both African and American experience and understandings. James Cone has stated that the five particular themes that characterize black theology are justice, liberation, hope, love, and suffering.[1]

The theme of *justice* is primary in black theology and, at first glance, seems more retributive than restorative. After all, God is known among African Americans as one who punishes evildoers who cannot escape such judgment—their wickedness will eventually catch up to them. Yet, as we progress through the other themes, one comes to see that they work together to culminate in a spirituality that holds the promise of reconciliation: suffering. Yes, African Americans hold a certainty of *liberation* for those oppressed by evildoers, particularly through the bondage of slavery, and the *hope* that derives from this certainty is based solely on God, who punishes evil and liberates the oppressed. Such trust in God's promises of liberation and justice is what gave black slaves the strength to maintain unity and even fight back against their oppressors. The theme of *love*, which is usually given priority in white theology, is seen directly in relation to these other three themes in black theology. Indeed, it is in viewing love through the lens of justice that the latter reaches beyond retribution and comes closer to Archbishop Tutu's vision of *Ubuntu.* As Cone states, "God's creation of all persons in the divine image bestows sacredness upon human beings and thus makes them the children of God. To violate any person's dignity is to transgress 'God's great law of love.'"[2] It is for this violation that God calls oppressors to account.

> *Suffering and death can be an experience not only of culmination but of starting again. In other words, it is not only a new way of looking at human life, but a new way of living it.*

Yet it is the theme of *suffering,* especially what results from violating God's law of love, that both brings this comprehensive vision of black theology full circle and propels it into a spirituality that can *heal.* African Americans know that suffering is a certainty that can only be addressed by a God of justice. Through Jesus's spirituality of living in communion with God, humanity is capable of being personally present in the relationships of the triune God. Our suffering joins Jesus's suffering and therefore God's. Jesus makes us see the spirituality that arises from his death as the mode of living, the essential disposition of the believer. Suffering and even death can be an experience not only of culmination but of starting again. In other words, it is not only a new way of looking at human life, but a new way of living it.

Becoming Saints

The work of the renowned African American mystic Howard Thurman helps us to understand this black spirituality, as it is grounded in suffering and death. In his 1963 essay "Suffering,"[3] Thurman writes, "The startling discovery is made that if there were no suffering there would be no freedom. . . . The ultimate logic of suffering, of course, lies in the fact of death. The particular quality of death is to be found in what it says about the future" (50). To understand suffering, therefore, one must see its context of death: "Death is seen as being an experience within Life, not happening to Life" (51). Thurman "recognizes that death, through its part in defining duration, does establish a form or aspect of life, and in so doing gives life a meaning and a purpose. It provides a measuring rod for values to be worked out within a particular time interval" (51). Such an interval could be described as the process of becoming a saint, one who continues to confirm life in the midst of a violent world. Thurman concludes that, "such confirmation of life in us is the work of the Holy Spirit of God" (53). But what does it mean to become a saint? Thurman suggests at least two practices.

First, to become a saint is to embody the presence of God in the world. Participating in this mystery requires ecstatic individuals who understand that God is not embodied in the caprice of individualism. Thurman states that the saint's God "must be more than his thought about God, more than his private needs, demands, or requirements" (52). Embodying the presence of God through the Holy Spirit enables the sufferer to overcome the meaningless of death. Thurman writes of the person who suffers:

> If the answer to his suffering is to face it and challenge it to do its worst because he knows that when it has exhausted itself it has only touched the outer walls of his dwelling place, this can only come to pass because he has found something big enough to contain all violences and violations—he has found that his life is rooted in a God who cares for him and cultivates his spirit, whose purpose is to bring to heel all the untutored, recalcitrant expressions of life. (53)

Second, to become a saint requires the ability not only to survive suffering but to move beyond suffering to a state of flourishing. Thurman articulates a Christian spirituality of sainthood through his own view of the flourishing life, which he calls "the grand fulfillment": "To seek to know how [one] may enter into such a grand fulfillment is the essence of all wisdom and the meaning of all human striving. Of course, [one] may be mistaken. But to be mistaken in such a grand and illumined undertaking is to go down to [the] grave with a shout" (54).

Thurman describes a man who appears to be saintlike, "yet there came a time when, in his encounter with personal suffering, he seemed stripped of every resource. His life became increasingly barren" (47). This movement from suffering to flourishing requires an initial stage of purgation, in which one engages the ultimate question of existence on account of coming in contact with one's mortality. Thurman observes that "suffering is given; it is part of the life contract that every living thing signs at the entrance" (50). Even though a person signs a contract to live and suffer, it is important to understand the meaning of suffering.

> *To become a saint requires the ability not only to survive suffering but to move beyond suffering to a state of flourishing.*

> But if the person comes to grips with his suffering by bringing to bear upon it all the powers of his mind and spirit, he moves at once into a vast but solitary arena. It is here that he faces the authentic adversary. He looks into the depth of the abyss of life and raises the ultimate question about the meaning of existence. He comes face to face with whatever is his conception of ultimate authority, his God. (45)

Suffering Creates Community

Survival in the dark night of the soul depends not so much on the ability of the individual to negotiate a way out; but on the awareness of his or her need to depend on others. In a strange way, suffering creates community as the wounded huddle close to one another in order to survive the next onslaught.

There is a fellowship of suffering as well as a community of sufferers. It is true that suffering tends to isolate the individual, to create a wall even within the privacy that imprisons him, to overwhelm him with self-preoccupation. It makes his spirit miserable in the literal sense of that word. Initially, it stops all outward flow of life and makes a virtue of the necessity for turning inward. Indeed, one of the ground rules of man's struggle with pain is the focusing of the energies of life at a single point. All of him that can be summoned is marshaled. This is true whether he is dealing with sheer physical pain or the more complex aspects of other dimensions of suffering. The pain gives his mind something else to think about and requires what approximates total attention. (44–45)

The community is important as individual sufferers seek resources outside of their individuality, a crucial search as the individual sufferer learns that pain is its own end. Thurman concludes, "Thus suffering may at times seem an end itself for generating energy in the spirit, as indeed it does. If the pain is great enough to lay siege to life and threaten it with destruction, a demand is made upon all one's resources. . . . It is important to hold in mind that this is the way of life—when life is attacked, it tends to rally all its forces to the defense" (46).

Thurman sheds light on the importance of community through African practices that illustrate individuals' ability to survive death on their own. This is why the African community must continue to pray for the dead, that they may keep moving beyond this life. The African focus on God the Creator is particularly helpful for articulating a spirituality capable of transcending suffering. Thurman states:

I cannot escape the necessity of concluding that the answer to suffering is to be found in experiencing in one's being the meaning of death. To state it categorically, it is to have one's innermost self or persona assured that the finality of death, which is the logic of all suffering, is itself contained in a more comprehensive finality of God Himself. Such a God is conceived as the creator of Life and the living substance, the Creator of existence itself and of all the time-and-space manifestations thereof. (53)

Christian spirituality is especially suited to provide communities with resources from which they may be able to move from suffering as its own end. Deep in the Christian faith is the understanding that suffering can be redemptive:

Despite the personal character of suffering, the sufferer can work his way through to community. . . . Sometimes he discovers through the ministry of his own burden a larger comprehension of his fellows, of whose presence he becomes aware in his darkness. They are companions along the way. The significance of this cannot be ignored or passed over. It is one of the consolations offered by the Christian religion in the centrality of the position given to the cross and to the suffering of Jesus Christ. (47)

Through the life of Christ some meaning is given to a world in which there are innocent who suffer. Suffering invites solidarity, calls forth dependence on the God of Life, and evokes our creative attempts at healing. Of the innocent who suffer, Thurman says, "Their presence in the world is a stabilizing factor, a precious ingredient maintaining the delicate balance that prevents humanity from plunging into the abyss. It is not surprising that in all the religions of mankind there is ever at work the movement to have the word made flesh, without being of the flesh" (49).

Embracing Death

It follows by extension, then, that the concept of Jesus's spirituality, grounded in suffering and death, can be applied to the problem of an enslaved church. For example, the response to death in the black church is radically different from what one might witness in most worship services in white churches. In the latter, an elaborate conspiracy of silence about death exists and everything is done to put it out of sight and mind, but in the African American context—particularly in rural areas—death is a stark reality with which everyone is familiar. Although death is a mystery, although it does violence to the weary one who clings to life, and although it is described in terms of "silence" and "immobility," it is nevertheless for black Christians somehow a new beginning. The consciousness of death is essential to spiritual growth; it fashions a kind of eternity for black Christians. In Jesus Christ, it is no longer difficult to die nobly. It is here that we learn how the church enslaved may discover resurrection or freedom through a renewed sense of spirituality, one that is not only based on survival but also on an open embrace of the reality of death.

The consciousness of death is essential to spiritual growth; it fashions a kind of eternity for black Christians.

But how does a church steeped in a colonial and slaveholding religion begin again? Thurman's profound description of "the movement of insight into a new idea," provides one suggestion:

> The impact upon the individual when he experiences himself as a human being is to regard himself as being of infinite worth. Such a sense of worth is not confined by narrow limits of the self so that worth may be determined by contrast with something or someone of less worth. No, this is a specious basis for ascertaining worth. Such a sense of worth is rooted in one's own consciousness which expands and expands until there is involved the totality of life itself. . . . To experience oneself as a human being is to feel life moving through one and claiming one as a part of it. It is like the movement of insight into a new idea or an aspect of truth. What initially is grasped by the mind and held there for meaning begins slowly or suddenly to hold the mind as if the mind itself is being thought by a vaster and greater Mind. It is like the thing that happens when you are trying to explain something to a child and you finally succeed in doing so. Then the child says, "I see." In that moment

you are no longer there in fact. The barrier that stood between the child's comprehension of the idea and the idea itself has been removed. There is a flowing together, as if the child and the idea were alone in all the universe.[4]

Ironically—as one gains individual, or personal insight, as if she "were alone in all the universe—Thurman teaches us that such insight does not come unless there is the mystery of the unseen community. In a story from his time in Nigeria, Thurman provides an example of how spirituality is communally dependent if it is to be understood at all.

> At the close of a lecture before the Press Club . . . I was invited to a small room for refreshments. I asked for a kind of soft drink called ginger beer. My host opened the bottle, poured a little on the floor as he said, "For my ancestors," and then he filled my glass. In this concept of the extended family . . . [t]o experience oneself as a human being is to know a sense of kinship with one's total environment and to recognize that it is this structural relationship that makes it possible for one to experience himself as a human being. Being white or black becomes merely incidental and is of no basic significance.[5]

Black Theology and African Theology

This perspective does not mitigate the fact that Western crimes against Africans in many cases resulted in a "rogue Christ" among these victims of colonialization constructed among them as a survival technique—a "new messiah" who would be for their people "what Jesus Christ is for the white man."[6] This is the distinction that is debated today between African American theologians and African theologians: namely, that black theology in America is a theology of liberation, but its context is still one of adapting to the Western world. African theology, on the other hand, is a theology of indigenization, or, more specifically, Africanization. Scholars like Josiah Young describe African theology as the effort of black Africans to make the Christian theology inherited from Europe congruent with African traditional religious thought. According to Young, African theology emphasizes a cultural perspective, whereas black theology in the United States (such as set forth by James Cone) emphasizes an ideological perspective: being black as the primary lens through which to interpret the gospel. An additional goal of African theologians is to indigenize the missionary church with African clergy and liturgies, African music, language, and movement.[7]

It must be said, as we noted in chapter 2, that the dangers that come from African Christians seeing the white Jesus of the Western missionaries are not necessarily reduced when Jesus is presented as an African. Yet, according to theologian Geoffrey Wainwright, "Black Africa is the next [territory] from which justice will best be done to the . . . tension-laden relation between the particularity and the universality of Jesus."[8] I agree with Wainwright and propose that we seek further to ease the particular/universal tension by thinking more in terms of culture than race in order to solve our inherent racial divisions. According to missiologist Lamin Sanneh, many oppressed peoples actually discovered a way to return to their cultural roots through the medium of Christianity itself.[9] Western influence and the colonial past cannot be undone, and African societies continue to evolve in a world context where the modern network of communications allows all cultural influence to be reciprocal, albeit unequal. There is no reason why particular local cultures should not continue to subsist within the universal framework as testimonies to the rich variety of God's work in human creation. As Thurman stated about his encounter with the indigenous people of Canada,

> *Black theology in America is a theology of liberation, but its context is still one of adapting to the Western world, while African theology is one of indigenization, or Africanization.*

In a conversation with three Indian chiefs in one of the Canadian provinces, I was deeply impressed particularly by the reply of one of them to the query, "Are you a Canadian and then an Indian, or are you an Indian and then a Canadian?" His reply, as it came through the interpreter, was essentially this: "I come from some miles near the Arctic circle in the north country. I live with the snow, the ice, the sharp wind in the winter; with the streams, the flowing waters, the sun and the blossoms in summer. These flow into me and I flow into them. They keep me and I keep them. I am a part of them and they are a part of me. I am not sure what you mean when you say Indian or Canadian.[10]

Locating Our Identity in Baptism

Just as the indigenous man Thurman spoke to countered standard expectations about his primary identity as either Indian or Canadian, so must we as Christians claim our identity in baptism rather than in race. We are followers of Jesus, first and last. Guided by such an understanding, we become a little less tempted to have the right words and answers to things, and instead become more eager to seek God's presence in all things. Because our theology is relative to a mystery that transcends our capacity to understand fully, we can have honest differences of interpretation with one another. When we gather together to probe this deep mystery that we sense at work in us, we can trust that where two or three are gathered together in true search for God, Christ's Spirit will guide us, even if our probing leaves us at different places of understanding or uncertainty at a given time. This leads us to a different understanding of God's goal for us—restoration.

> To claim baptism as the locus of our primary identity, we need to confess that our rites of initiation into the nature of God are unsatisfactory and need to be changed.

To claim baptism as the locus of our primary identity, we need to confess that our rites of initiation into the nature of God are unsatisfactory and need to be changed. For example, in other cultures there are rites of passage that recognize the adolescent's special status of being in transition, but in our Western Christian culture, what would this transition be—from what to what? In the West, we seem to have settled for a simplistic, consumeristic answer in which a kind of least-common-denominator spirituality gives all access to the nature of God while demanding little of the seeker. Why is such a "spirituality" more popular these days than the institutional church? One answer is the early church's understanding that Christian baptism signified a death on one hand, and resurrection on the other. Those who were baptized understood death in a deeply personal sense and not just in some allegorical manner. Christian baptism has now lost much of its life-altering significance, given the rise of civil religion and Christianity's own decent into individualism.

Spiritual writer Maggie Ross offers an interesting response to this question of why spirituality is more popular than the institutional church in her book *Pillars of Flame*. Ross wants to recover the strong concept of baptism's unique spiritual character—capable of substantial, fully committed existence in a world such as this. Baptism is the initiatory process into a living spirituality that can animate the church. The baptized are those who take special vows to live out their vocation more fully in the world. Ross writes:

> In the United States, the ... Church has hundreds of people inappropriately seeking ordination because they need some way of consecrating their lives, and although they know better intellectually, the present-day trivialization of baptism means that their baptismal vows do not signify the life-and-death commitment they wish to make. Baptism is cheap these days. What ... [minister] is not happy to have another dues-paying member on the rolls or a larger body count to report ... at the end of the year? The average member of a congregation seems to have made the haziest sort of commitment—if there is any sense of commitment at all—and is quite happy to remain in the role of a second-class

citizen. But this basking in ecclesial sloth is not what Christianity is about.[11]

Rightly understood, our baptism subverts our pallid Christianity because inevitably God's nature and that of the powers and principalities of this world find their central dynamics in serious tension. Consequently, we must choose which central dynamic will become the basis for our lifestyle. We posit that this central dynamic may be found in Jesus's Sermon on the Mount.

The Sermon on the Mount

The expectations of moral and ethical living in the Sermon on the Mount are so high that some have dismissed them as being completely unrealistic or have projected their fulfillment to the future kingdom of God. There is no doubt, however, that Jesus (and Matthew) gave the sermon as a standard for all Christians, realizing that its requirements cannot be met under our own power. The demands of Jesus in the Sermon on the Mount can be met only in the living initiation into the nature of God discovered through the special revelation of Jesus. Hence we define Christian spirituality as the created life of human beings in which mutuality of relationships between God and among all persons is demonstrated for us in the life, death, resurrection, and ascension of Jesus Christ.

The Sermon on the Mount teaches us that we, who call ourselves the church, are initiated into the nature of God, not because we share a common rationality, but because we find ourselves to be people who follow Jesus. We are people defined in the middle of an adventure in which our human identity is not as fully formed as Jesus's humanity. And although Jesus is fully God and fully human, our discipleship is a process of being made *more human*. Our humanity is dependent upon the Christian narrative of Jesus to tell us who we are—what our real and ultimate nature is. If we do not see and hear ourselves defined through the life, death, resurrection, and ascension of Jesus, then we naturally fall into a sophistry in which spirituality is seen as a state of being, abstracted from contingencies of history. In such a spirituality, people cannot help but appear as an unconnected series of actions lacking continuity and unity. And this is where justice enters the picture. If there is no true humanity, then justice becomes unintelligible.

> *Christian spirituality is the created life of human beings in which mutuality of relationships between God and among all persons is demonstrated for us in the life, death, resurrection, and ascension of Jesus Christ.*

Individualistic senses of Christian spirituality, disconnected from the Christian story, will continue to be caricatures from Monty Python movies in which the expression of that story can only be a comedy. If we do not take seriously the demand for integrity between the nature of God shown in Christ and our own lifestyle, then the church decends into the demonic in which we confuse the nature of God with the power of death. In other words, we can easily fall victim to the worldview that our lives are our own and that we live because of the accidents of nature and that we must maximize our existence before we simply return to primordial matter.

What we proclaim as a church is a much different narrative—that even when we do return to nature as dust, Jesus has somehow effected the resurrection not just of our souls but of our bodies. Somehow, when we die, we become like inanimate seeds, bodies planted in the earth; and just as we can hardly imagine the massive tree resulting from an inanimate seed, we can barely imagine the life that results from our return to the dust. In fact, Jesus proclaims in the Sermon on the Mount that we are to be happy, even in the face of powers of death. Only Jesus, however, truly models beatitude, or happiness, so we often fall short and are exposed as modeling manipulative attitudes. Instead of interiorizing our Christian spirituality, we need to remember that the message of the Sermon cannot be abstracted from the Messenger. If Jesus is the Messiah, then he has made it possible for us to live in accordance with the Sermon through his death and resurrection. Jesus has made it possible for all of us saints. The Sermon on the Mount, and the Beatitudes especially, are the forms of his life; and his death and resurrection form the prism through which the Sermon is interpreted. In short, the Sermon does not appear impossible to people who are called to a life of discipleship that requires them to contemplate their own life and death in the light of the cross of Christ.

What Is Christian Spirituality?

Our aim has been for you to reflect and ask with us what spirituality means—more particularly, what *Christian* spirituality means. Therefore, there is no such thing as an unadulterated spirituality, and the disabled church of today has perhaps narrowed our vision of the Christian life and spirituality. In our hope of securing beatitude among people of great despair, we Christians have often overlooked the most important contributions that Christian convictions make for the moral life. A watered-down spirituality makes irrelevant the essential Christian convictions about the nature of God and God's providence for creation through God's calling of Israel and the life of Jesus. Often, our "beliefs" about such matters are relegated to some separate "religious aspects" of our lives, where they make little difference to our moral existence. Yet, finally, our Christian commitment must be fulsome and practical if it is to be real. As theologian Stanley Hauerwas states, "Communities teach us what kind of intentions are appropriate if we are to be the kind of person appropriate to living among these people. Thus questions of what we ought to be are necessary background for questions of what we ought to do."[12]

To nurture such a powerful and engaged commitment, we want to focus on the need for a mystical, contemplative spirituality that helps to shape our self-understanding as baptized children of God, living in the community known as church.

CHAPTER 10

A Practice of Contemplation

Nurturing a deeper faith through contemplation cleanses prejudice, renews our minds, and engages us with each other.

Embracing our identities as baptized Christians, as people who live within a culture of the kingdom of God, means that we need to reach beyond categories that divide and stereotype us, that confine us in individualistic self-concepts apart from community. To develop this kind of spirituality, we need to reach a new understanding of the vocation of prayer. Without such a transformation, this vocation runs the risk of being or becoming artificial. If one thinks he or she "has arrived" in the spiritual life or has perfected spiritual being, then there is little incentive to pray as Jesus taught us in such an authentic and humble way (Luke 18:10-15). If there is no such humility in prayer, the spiritual life becomes individualistic and barren. We advocate a different path, one of real growth and engagement.

Seeking a Mystical Christianity

We assert that black Christians along with white Christians require a Christianity that is mystical. Only by surrendering to the Holy Spirit and allowing the Christ who comes to redefine us in the context of contemplative praying will we escape the cultural tyranny that religion often creates. We need to be transformed by the Holy Spirit as the apostle Paul tells us in

116

Romans 12, rather than transforming God into our own image. To be free from the psychological and sociological enslavement that comes from cultural Christianity, those who would be followers of the true Jesus must go through a process of cleansing from God and deep spiritual meditation. It would be wise for Christians, both white and black, to read up on the writings of pre-Reformation saints such as Ignatius, Francis, Teresa, John of the Cross, and Julian of Norwich. Perhaps, through these ancient saints, people of all racial groups might learn how to allow the Christ who is within each of us to expand and purge us of the cultural trappings of our religious ideas. To be pure of heart, in the way Jesus talks about in the Beatitudes, is to be a people who are cleansed of racist images of God and imbued with the Spirit working within. This is what Paul is talking about in Romans 12:1-2:

> *To be free from the psychological and sociological enslavement that comes from cultural Christianity, those who would be followers of the true Jesus must go through a process of cleansing from God and deep spiritual meditation.*

> I appeal to you therefore, brothers and sisters, by the mercies of God, to present your bodies as a living sacrifice, holy and acceptable to God, which is your spiritual worship. Do not be conformed to this world, but be transformed by the renewing of your minds, so that you may discern what is the will of God— what is good and acceptable and perfect.

Both blacks and whites need a renewal of their minds, and this does not come simply through an intellectual process; it comes through contemplative praying. It comes when the Holy Spirit transforms us from within, destroying the religious conceptualizations that were provided by the culture, and makes us into new creations. As Paul writes, "So if anyone is in Christ, there is a new creation: everything old has passed away; see, everything has become new!" (2 Cor. 5:17).

It is not enough to escape political and economic enslavement, as important as deliverance from these forces is. Psychological and sociological deliverance, which can only come under the power of the Holy Spirit, is also necessary. If we seem a bit Pentecostal when we talk this way—so be it. It is about time that the church recognize that without the miraculous transformation of the mind, soul, and heart, the truth about God will never be known. It is that truth that will make us free.

Making Room for the Spirit

Breaking down the church stereotypes that become self-fulfilling prophecies will require iconoclastic approaches. One can point to both negative and positive examples of breaking the paralyzing tendencies of a racist church and world. For instance, Evangelicals need to make more room for the transforming effects of the work of the Holy Spirit. A survey of Evangelical churches will reveal that the Pentecostal congregations—having a strong emphasis on charismatic influences—are the most likely to be racially integrated. Time and time again, visits to Pentecostal churches will reveal a surprising rate of fellowship across racial lines in these worshiping communities.

For those who don't embrace Pentecostalism, we advocate a contemplative form of spirituality that can go a long way to overcoming racial divisions. For instance, Tony gets up every morning a half hour before he needs to and spends time focusing on Jesus. In this half hour of prayer he does not ask God for anything except to be invaded by the Holy Spirit. He says the name of Jesus over and over again, driving out of his consciousness thoughts of anything else. Such contemplative practice does for him what is talked about in the old African American spiritual, "Woke up this morning with my mind stayed on Jesus."

As we noted in chapter 2, contemplative practices of the particular form we advocate here are seldom found in the black church, in part because of the need to create a specifically black church identity over against the white, hegemonic version of Christianity.[1] Indeed, it is somewhat ironic that we would advocate that African American Christians come to a new appreciation of spiritual writers such as Ignatius and Teresa so closely identified with white Christianity. Yet, as we recover our African heritage and embrace the concept of *Ubuntu*, clearly

> *Breaking down the chuch stereotypes that become self-fulfilling prophecies will require iconoclastic approaches.*

there is no reason that the church as a whole cannot embrace what these spiritual masters have to teach us.

We believe that contemplative spirituality is an important means for overcoming racism because of its potential to build the kind of unity that typifies communities that are part of the body of Christ. By concentrating on Christ alone, to quote an old hymn, "The things of earth grow strangely dim." We need to drive back the animals of death—the animals being the hundred and one things that consume the a person's consciousness upon awakening each morning. These strange thoughts and concerns must be driven out of the mind in order to create what Celtic Christians once called "a thin place." This particular state of being is one in which the walls separating the individual from God are so thin that the Holy Spirit seems to come through and envelop the believer completely. The barriers that so often exist between the believer and God are washed away by the Spirit's work. Bathed in the Spirit (again to quote an old hymn), "I ask no dream, no prophet's ecstasy, just take the deadness of my soul away." In such a contemplative state, Tony sometimes senses the Holy Spirit invading his being, which exercises a transforming effect on his personality: "Something very mystical happens to me. I look at the world in a whole new way. What is most important is that I can confront other people to the extent that the Holy Spirit possesses me. In so doing, I have the superior awareness that Christ is waiting to be loved in the other."

Such spirituality has the obvious potential to break down racial barriers because people who are possessed by the Spirit look into the eyes of someone of another race they sense Jesus in that person. It becomes impossible to reject that person. How can a Christian reject another if that other person is the sacramental presence of Christ? Is not such rejection a rejection of Christ himself? Put simply, if, under the power of the Holy Spirit, an individual sees Jesus in the other, then rejecting such a person is impossible. Indeed, for anyone full of the Spirit, the words of Jesus, "in as much as you have done it to the least of these, you have done it unto me," take on special meaning. Now interpersonal relationships, especially across racial lines, are open to transformation.

Contemplative Prayer and Community

Unlike our individualistic society in Western culture, in which the self presupposes the need to be alone, we argue that true contemplative prayer leads to community. Since we are both individuals and community, a synergy exists in which our individuality is dependent upon healthy community. This is what we think the image of God is—not so much male or female, black or white, but the dependency between individuality and community—in other words, the Trinity. God so loved the world that, even though we were unworthy of love, God granted us salvation in which we could live. Forgiveness is a perfectly free gift of Jesus. And grace transforms the sinner, for God's love makes the unlovely lovely indeed. When we pray (contemplating life in the spirit), we are often awestruck by the impossible beauty of this grace— we actually experience a love we know we do not deserve. We are changed by the impossible truths we meet in our experience, as we become ever-new creatures.

Since we are both individuals and community, a synergy exists in which our individuality is dependent upon healthy community.

Of course, it is important to recognize that not all Christians are equally drawn to a mystical form of belief and practice. As spiritual director and teacher Corinne Ware has shown (drawing from the work of the late Episcopal spiritual writer Urban T. Holmes III), there are at least four major spiritual types—identified by their focus—make up most Christian churches: (1) *head* (rationalism and theology); (2) *heart* (feelings and holiness); (3) *kingdom* (action and changing society); and (4) *mystic* (interior world and prayer).[2] We do not list these to further categorize people; rather, we simply wish to demonstrate that the *mystic* dimension is often neglected in both black and white churches. Many mainline Protestant congregations are typified by a *head* spirituality; as our typology in chapter 6 shows, many black churches are focused on *heart* forms of belief. And both black and white Christians who

> *The dynamistic presence of the Holy Spirit in the life of Christians can purge our hearts, minds, and souls of the demons of racist attitudes.*

work for racial reconciliation are often drawn to Christianity's *kingdom* forms in their genuine desire to change society and usher in the reign of God.

Those who embrace mystical spirituality take people very seriously. They are aware of personalized demonic forces at work in the world and know that these forces not only are able to possess individuals, but can also control social structures so that they become instruments of evil. Such structures can destroy people when controlled by evil spirits, and this reality cannot be ignored when dealing with racism. Most African Americans have no problem understanding this kind of thought concerning structural evil. They are all too familiar with demonic forces, not only in personal lives but in social systems. Just as they have seen God at work in the world, so they have seen Satan at work perverting all of society through his minions.

The dynamistic presence of the Holy Spirit in the life of Christians can purge our hearts, minds, and souls of the demons of racist attitudes. Racism is so implanted in the psyche of human beings that some say that racism can never be extinguished—those people embrace the politics of resignation that we described in chapter 1. But such a miracle is possible with God's presence. Any attempt to overcome racism simply by rational evaluation, as important as that is, will not accomplish what ultimately needs to be done. Both black and white people need new hearts and minds, which can only be created miraculously by being possessed by God's Spirit. A spirituality of racial reconciliation will not occur overnight. But it should begin now. The first effects of a spirituality of racial reconciliation are already present and are even celebrated around the world.

As we move into a postmodern era, we must recognize that the rationalistic approach to the Christian faith—a predominant characteristic of white Christianity—is being seriously called into question. An emerging worldview that recognizes the limitations of modernity, which only accepted as truth what could be verified by reason and science, is having an impact on Christians everywhere. Even those in the secular academic community are readily admitting a new humility that provides room for truth that transcends positivistic ways of looking at things. Truth that transcends the empirical world, truth that is witnessed to through the life of the church is increasingly recognized. In the same way, we are also recognizing that the emotion- and action-oriented forms of Christianity are not adequate in and of themselves to transform the enslaved church. In closing we will look at some wholistic ways that the church can be transformed into a reconciled community.

CHAPTER 11

A Church of Reconciliation

*Reconciling love can find many ways and means
and places to aid human flourishing.*

In the previous chapter we advocated for both black and white Christians to embrace an often neglected contemplative form of spirituality as a means to effect racial reconciliation. Yet we also noted that many Christians express their spirituality primarily in ways other than the contemplative—through thought and study, through feelings and experience, through action and working for social change. In our final chapter we wish to offer three further constructive routes, taking account of these other spirituality styles, that both blacks and whites use to overcome racism and embrace a spirituality of restoration.

Accepting Black Leadership

In the postmodern world, Christians are looking for forms of religion that give them spiritual experiences that can be felt, appealing to a *heart* spirituality. It is obvious that such an emerging attitude is consonant with black religion, which has always had an intensely emotional quality in its worship services. In the black community there is a difference between "going to church" and "having church." People feel like they are "having church" when they feel spiritual ecstasy during the morning worship hour. White Christians are increasingly seeking what has been normative in black

Christianity. Pentecostalism, which had its modern resurgence under the leadership of the black pastor of the Azusa mission in the Los Angeles area in the early part of the twentieth century, has now had an impact on almost all of Christianity. Contemporary worship services are becoming popular alternatives to traditional forms of worship in white churches across the country, and the music of Pentecostalism has penetrated the most staid white denominations of the land. Such spiritual expressions have an affinity with what has typified black worship over the last couple of centuries.

> *Whenever white people attend black churches and experience their spontaneous and relevant worship, they almost always report how much more they enjoyed those worship services than what they normally experience in their own churches.*

The spiritual ecstasy that defines this contemporary worship in white churches has its roots in the context of most black churches. Contemporary worship is about spontaneity and relevance, two descriptions that readily identify styles of the black church. When white people attend black churches and experience their spontaneous and relevant worship, they almost always report how much more they enjoyed those worship services than what they normally experience in their own churches. When Tony talks to his white friends who have had worship experiences in black churches, he often hears them say things like:

- "I really felt the presence of God when I was with those people."
- "The service was more than two hours, but it felt like ten minutes."
- "It was so exciting."
- "I came away with my spirits lifted in ways that I never have experienced with my own congregation."

Tony usually responds to such remarks with a simple question, "If God is so real and worship is so exciting in the black congregation, why do you continue to worship in that white church where you hold your membership?" Those he questions almost seem stunned by such inquiry and usually say something like, "I never thought of doing that," in such a way that suggests they might seriously consider that possibility.

Young people criticize mainline white churches through the simple declaration that they find their worship services "boring." Yet these same young people seldom, if ever, critique what happens when they attend "mainline" black churches. All of this is to suggest that the time has come for white Christians to ask themselves whether or not the time has come to welcome black church leaders as their worship guides. Not only would this foster racial reconciliation, it just might be a major step toward the revitalization of white Christianity, especially as it exists in mainline denominationalism.

Developing Self-Critical Approaches to Multiculturalism

The hard work of following Christ requires faithfulness to the ongoing flourishing of God's creation. We do not turn the other cheek because it is the way to avoid a fight, but because we have been discipled always to think and act in ways congruent with helping creation to flourish. The notion of transformation, in which mostly white and economically privileged people actually learn to share power, is not just for the sake of people of color and economically underprivileged people. It is also for the sake of those in power, who finally come to understand what it means to flourish. Those in power know deep in their bones the paradox that being wealthy does not itself make life worth living. Until all move to an understanding of structural and deep-seated inequities in our societies, there will be no sense of flourishing. Multicultural education expert Sonia Nieto explains:

> Caring cannot be taught. This is especially true in courses that
> focus solely on the head, removing social issues to the sphere

of intellectual problems. But caring can be modeled, and community service learning is one of the few places in the academy where this is most likely to happen. Unfortunately, even in community service learning courses, the notion of caring is often perceived only as an individual concern for the "unfortunate" and "underprivileged," and this perception does little to confront the institutionalized nature of inequality. But when an ethic of care is modeled within a framework of inquiry about broad-based inequality and oppression . . . the potential to change hearts as well as heads is enhanced.[1]

How do we effect deep understanding about inequities in society through the ancient truth given to us by Christ? We must first model truth before speaking about it. We must worship truth before doing theology. We must first feed the hungry, clothe the naked, visit the prisoner, and heal the sick, and then talk about who is or is not going to heaven. We must first build hospitals, schools, and shelters and then talk about Christian missions. Living first into the model Christ set for us is how we get at the problem of systemic inequities. This model becomes a prophetic framework for understanding the sacred.

Upon living into Christ's model of service for the sake of flourishing for all of creation, the crucial question becomes: How does one relate well in a multicultural context? In other words, what does a successful model of a flourishing society look like? If we know what it looks like then we can model ourselves after it.

The model of flourishing that we envision reflects a particular understanding of community. Christian educator Parker Palmer describes community as the "capacity for relatedness within individuals—relatedness not only to people, but to events in history, to nature, to the world of ideas, and yes, to things of the spirit."[2] Palmer's is yet another voice that helps us to see the capacity for interrelatedness as the solution to the individualism of our day. Religious and theological discourse proves important in shaping our notions of what constitutes community and what citizenship looks like in such community. It is interesting to note that even such secular theorists as R. A. Rhoads see this problem, "Notions of citizenship often are vague and need to be anchored in a clear understanding of what kind of society we desire. There can be no vision of citizens or citizenship without a vision of society."[3]

In light of the above definition of community, the question becomes, What constitutes community service that is not patronizing? This question points toward ideological considerations behind any notion of community service and multicultural education. What moves such ideological considerations as religion and theology beyond "charity" work is the intentional and critical focus on combining theoretical and practical work that envisions a flourishing society. Since many of us who offer to serve the oppressed generally have more advantages than those who are served, it is difficult to articulate a flourishing community without addressing the problem of unearned privilege. In other words, for many of us, the problem becomes how to dislodge the perception that community service is missionary work. For those in secular settings, such a problem raises deep ambivalence. Ultimately, such ambivalence may lead us Christians to re-evaluate our community service experiences, which have shown mixed results at best. What we know deep in our bones, however, is that Jesus offers us lessons on how to create experiences for oppressor and oppressed alike that positively influence mutual liberation from structural evil.

How do we effect deep understanding about inequities in society through the ancient truth given to us by Christ? We must first model truth before speaking about it.

Practitioners and theorists in multicultural work need to engage in dialogue about how spiritual work and multicultural work can be explicitly combined so that both reinforce a critical approach. Combining spiritual and multicultural work is important because, despite the conflicting rhetoric against and for multiculturalism, Christian workers in community service centers are among the few who analyze the relationship between diversity issues and God's plan of salvation for all of creation. In the face of overwhelming social and religious crises, as exemplified by the

9/11 attacks and the Iraq war, such work is especially pertinent for us today.

The challenge is how Christian and other religious workers can discern whether their work is successful or more damaging. How do we know when our work in the soup kitchen is empowering or patronizing? This is especially the challenge among those of us typically seen as living in ivory towers or distant suburbs, who no longer know if "charity work" is still a good phrase. Nieto clarifies the distinction between charity work and community service. Charity work implies "detached beneficence," whereas community service "conjures up images of doing good deeds in impoverished, disadvantaged (primarily Black and Brown) communities by those (mostly White people) who are wealthier and more privileged."[4] The successful response to the challenge of knowing whether we are doing more good than harm, we think, can only be known by maintaining a balance between thinking hard about multicultural contexts and working faithfully in those contexts to which God calls us. In other words, we are most successful and not damaging to others when we practice what we preach.

> *Since many of us who offer to serve the oppressed are generally those who have more advantages than those who are served, it is difficult to articulate a flourishing community without addressing the problem of unearned privilege.*

We have much to gain by practicing the integrity between theory and action when it comes to antiracism work. When Christians work against racism, our task is to explicitly address how God's creation flourishes. The work of multicultural consultant Valerie Batts is again helpful here. Batts believes that multicultural reality must overcome four levels of racism:

1.   *Personal:* Racism is bias or prejudice; here one notes conscious or unconscious attitudes that whites are superior and that blacks and other people of color are inferior

2.   *Interpersonal:* Behaviors based on conscious or unconscious biased assumptions about self and other become interpersonal manifestations of racism

3. *Institutional or Systemic:* How policies, practices, laws, styles, rules, or procedures function to the advantage of the dominant group and to the disadvantage of people of color

4. *Cultural:* European-American and Western cultural preferences are considered correct and "beautiful," and standards of appropriate action, thought, and expression of a particular group are perceived either overtly or subtly as negative or inferior.[5]

Unless we address all these levels of racism and model multicultural reality, there will be no such reality as the flourishing of creation. As we learn from our examination of *Ubuntu,* the flourishing of creation depends on how well we learn to be interdependent. The way that societies learn to flourish is through recognizing, celebrating, understanding, and appreciating difference on each level: personal, interpersonal, institutional, and cultural.

Imagine, for instance, a white supervisor in a workplace who is confused as to why the black and Latino/a coworkers she oversees perceive her as racist when she feels she treats everybody the same. Although sincere in her desire to deal with all her employees fairly, when she examines her behavior she realizes that she has been unconsciously working from a *personal* assumption that since her coworkers of color had been brought up in communities different from her own (and presumably less adequate), they are thus inferior. Her *interpersonal* behavior toward these employees is not only disempowering to them, it leaves them feeling helpless and less capable. Again, she is genuine in her desire to correct rather than perpetuate past inequities; nevertheless, her interactions with her employees of color implies to them that she regards them as second-class citizens. Thus, these employees feel they are being set up either to accept these attitudes of inferiority and helplessness or to reject their supervisor and what she represents to them. In her efforts "not to see color" she nevertheless experiences inchoate feelings of guilt, disgust, or fear that she has dismissed or converted into pity for the "victims" of systemic oppression, avoiding openly racist people whenever she can. Yet her personal and interpersonal responses unintentionally work to perpetuate dysfunctional interracial behavior. This is reinforced on an institutional level by the mostly white culture of her workplace where many staff have little contact with people of color in their personal lives outside of work. The *cultural* norm of this workplace has long been defined by white, male, Protestant, middle-class, middle-aged, heterosexual, and physically able standards, and change is slow.

The experience of this woman is replicated in millions of situations across America everyday—in workplaces, in educational institutions, in neighborhoods, and in churches. It is incumbent upon white people to regularly examine themselves, their actions, and their attitudes to uncover when and where they may be perpetuating racism on any of these four levels. Moreover, white people need their black brothers and sisters to help them to recognize when they may be unintentionally acting and thinking in racist ways. At the same time, African Americans need to recognize when they may be acceding to such behaviors and attitudes and show courage in calling others to account.

> *White people need their black brothers and sisters to help them to recognize when they may be unintentionally acting and thinking in racist ways.*

Speaking the Truth in Love

If white Christians and black Christians are to establish intimate fellowship with each other, it is essential that they speak the truth to each other in love. The hostilities that African Americans have toward white people should not be covered up and treated as nonexistent. Cornel West, in his book *Race Matters,* contends that certain African American leaders, notably Martin Luther King Jr., have given to black people a kind of messianic complex in which they see themselves as innocent victims of white oppression.[6] It is far too easy to blame all the evils of racial discrimination on what white people have done to black people, and to do so in a way that leaves black people with a sense that there is nothing at all wrong with them and that the fault for everything that is wrong in their lives can be laid at the feet of white oppressors.

If the German sociologist Georg Sorel were alive today, he would likely argue that simply blaming the oppressor is itself an instrument of oppression. If the destiny of the oppressed people lies solely in the hands of the oppressors, then there is nothing the oppressed people can do to gain liberation. Their destiny lies only in the hands of those who have made their lives miserable. Things will only improve insofar as the oppressors repent and changes their attitudes and behavioral patterns. The problem, according to Sorel, is that it is not likely that the oppressors, who are enjoying the benefits of their injustice, are ever going to repent.

Karl Marx picked up this theme by contending that those who have power never give it up willingly; instead, it has to be wrested from them through violence. We reject violence as a means dealing with the wrongs that stem from slavery and have continued to haunt America today through systemic practices of racial discrimination. But there is still much to change in the white community. Black brothers and sisters can help white people understand the subtleties of much of the oppression that white people exercise daily. Blacks can help whites better understand the latent racism whites seldom recognize in themselves and that blacks perceive as they experience the results of that racism in their everyday lives. This is the "politics of education" that we advocated in chapter 1.

> *If the destiny of the oppressed people lies solely in the hands of the oppressors, then there is nothing the oppressed people can do to gain liberation. Their destiny lies only in the hands of those who have made their lives miserable.*

On the other hand, white churches can be helpful to African Americans without being patronizing, but only if they are willing to be honest in their dialogue with their black brothers and sisters in Christ. In public, whites generally work overtime to make politically correct statements lest unless black people "play a race card" against them. White Christians need to speak honestly and tell black people truths about themselves that African Americans seldom admit openly.

One way we might begin is to recognize that slavery existed in America, not just because of the evils inherent in the white race, but also because of the evils inherent among black Africans. That means that we must acknowledge the complicity of African blacks with white slave traders. White people were not the only ones who captured black people in Africa and made them available to slave traders. Tribal wars in Africa often resulted in conquered peoples being enslaved by other blacks and sold to white slave merchants, who brought them across the ocean to the "new world." In other words, slavery existed not just because of the evils of white slave traders, but also because black tribes conquered and sold other human beings to the highest bidders. Those who would make whites the sole culprits for that evil practice must come to see things in a broader perspective to be truthful.

> *Slavery existed not just because of the evils of white slave traders, but also because black tribes conquered and sold other human beings to the highest bidders.*

Another criticism that black people need to hear from whites is regularly shared when black people are not around but seldom expressed when black people are present: African Americans in today's world often do not take advantage of the opportunities that are made available to them. For instance, it is time for black leaders to call young people to accountability as students and press them to take advantage of the opportunities that have become available to them over the last few decades. Black church leaders should be demanding a high level of accountability in the academic activities of the students in their congregations.

Many white people, when blacks are not around, often bristle at the behavior of African American employees who hold jobs as result of affirmative action programs. William Julius Wilson, the famous African American sociologist, reports that many employers are afraid to hire African Americans because they fear being reported to a human relations committee or civil rights commission if they reprimand black workers for not performing as they should. This angers many white people and they wish that leaders in the African

American community—including church leaders—would begin to hold black people responsible for how they behave in the workplace and stop blaming the white establishment for all of the problems that black people experience in business and industry.

Tony knows of a black church in Minneapolis whose pastor helps to secure employment for people in his congregation with a very high level of success. To accomplish this, the pastor goes to the church member's potential employer and guarantees that if the person creates any serious problem in the new job or fails to measure up to job expectations, he as pastor and the rest of the congregation will handle the problem and hold that person accountable. It is easy to criticize this practice and point out the racist implications of black employees being treated differently than are white employees. Nevertheless, it is one attempt to create a sense of accountability within the African American community that many whites believe needs to be established.

> *It is time for black leaders to call young people to accountability as students and press them to take advantage of the opportunities that have become available to them over the last few decades.*

If there is going to be reconciliation, there must be accountability so that white people can tell each other what is wrong in their attitudes and behavior and black people do the same among themselves. What is more, each group, if honest, can help the other to see flaws and shortcomings that the other groups do not often see in itself. Effective church leadership, creating "safe spaces" to speak the truth in love, can foster this process. Restorative justice processes, as we have already described in chapter 8, can also help create systems of accountability.

Being Evangelical about Social Justice in Practical Ways

We close our book with the story of Tony's son, Bart Campolo, which illustrates well the points we have just made. Over the past six years, with Tony's encouragement, Bart has developed a program called Mission Year. Through that program, hundreds of young people have been recruited to spend a year living, working, and serving in urban neighborhoods. Young people in the program are predominantly white, but the neighborhoods they work in are mostly black and, in some cases, Latino. These young people are divided into teams of six, with at least five teams to a city. Each team lives in an urban neighborhood and becomes affiliated with an ethnic church, usually African American. They do not exercise any leadership in the churches with which they affiliate because they do not want to usurp leadership from indigenous people. They simply attend worship and support the pastor in every way possible. Each team belongs to a specific church, whose pastor is responsible for the spiritual nurturing of the team members. Each of the cities has a professionally trained city director who helps educate the team members in the sociology and psychology of urban life. The students read books that will give them some idea as to what is going on in their neighborhoods and the causes of the social problems they find there. In addition, these young people spend most of their time becoming personally acquainted with their neighbors, praying with people and for people.

Each Mission Year volunteer is required to complete forty hours of ministry a week. Twenty of these hours are designated for door-to-door visitation. Whenever possible, members of the churches they are serving are asked to go along on these visits. Following the biblical model based on Jesus's words in Matthew 10:5-15, they go out two by two, asking for nothing more than to be a blessing to those whom they visit:

> These twelve Jesus sent out with the following instructions: "Go nowhere among the Gentiles, and enter no town of the Samaritans, but go rather to the lost sheep of the house of Israel. As you go, proclaim the good news, 'The kingdom of heaven has come near.' Cure the sick, raise the dead, cleanse the lepers, cast out demons. You received without payment; give without payment.

Take no gold, or silver, or copper in your belts, no bag for your journey, or two tunics, or sandals, or a staff; for laborers deserve their food. Whatever town or village you enter, find out who in it is worthy, and stay there until you leave. As you enter the house, greet it. If the house is worthy, let your peace come upon it; but if it is not worthy, let your peace return to you. If anyone will not welcome you or listen to your words, shake off the dust from your feet as you leave that house or town. Truly I tell you, it will be more tolerable for the land of Sodom and Gomorrah on the day of judgment than for that town.

When a Mission Year worker knocks on a door and gets an answer, he or she simply says:

We're from the church down the street and we've made a commitment to pray for every family in the immediate neighborhood. We very much want to pray for you and ask God's blessing on you and those who live with you. We're not selling anything or trying to get you to come to our church—though if you would come we'd be very happy. We're not even trying to convert you to anything. We just want to pray *for* you and with you. Can we do that? We don't have to come into your house or anything like that—we can pray God's blessing on you and those who live with you right here while we stand on your doorstep.

The surprised and skeptical neighbor usually says yes, even if he or she is of another religion or an agnostic. There is usually a guarded but positive response like, "I suppose it wouldn't hurt." There will be follow-up visits that can lead to the kinds of dialogue that bring people into personal relationships with Christ, but initially all that is offered is a prayer of blessing.

Before leaving a given family, each Mission Year team is likely to ask this question: "Tonight, after dinner, we're going to have a time of prayer. We pray for those we visited during the day. Are there any special concerns or needs that you have that we should bring before the Lord when we go to prayer this evening?" It is amazing how many people respond by being honest and open about their needs:

- "My daughter's pregnant and she needs help."
- "My youngest child is on drugs, failing in school, and wants to drop out. I don't know what to do."
- "My husband is out of work and can't find a job."

At the end of the day when the team gets together and prays for these people, they do one thing more. They go over the list of social services available in the community to see if there are people nearby who can help:

- In response to the girl who's pregnant, someone is apt to say, "That Catholic church down the street has a crisis pregnancy center; let's be in touch with them and see if they can do something to help that young woman."
- Someone says, "We can help that kid on drugs by calling Teen Challenge, the Pentecostal group that does such a great job of helping kids overcome their drug addictions. Let's call them and ask them to send somebody over to that house on Felton Street where that boy has such trouble with drugs."
- Someone else might say, "The woman whose husband does not have a job can be helped. There ought to be some help from the YMCA—they run a job placement service Let's call the YMCA and tell them to send someone over to see that man."

What is obvious is that there is no need to create new ministries. For those who live in the inner city, enough ministries already exist. The problem is that those who need help from those ministries seldom seek them out. Often they do not take the initiative and go for the help that they require. But then, Jesus never said that we should expect people to come to us; rather, Jesus told us that we should go to them.

The Mission Year program provides a means for white people to minister in the black community without being oppressive. Instead of usurping leadership or creating ministries that compete with indigenous ministries, the Mission Year workers connect people in need with ministries that already exist. Those ministries are usually in the hands of African American leaders who are thrilled to have their services marketed so effectively by the Mission Year workers who go door to door seeking to minister to everyone in the neighborhood.

It is not surprising that the NAACP gave special recognition to the work of a Mission Year team at their annual awards ceremony. They declared that Mission Year had discovered a way for white people to work in black communities without a spirit of superiority and condescension. In the end, Mission Year workers lend incredible support to ministries of African Americans who have worked hard to establish and struggle to maintain ministries in the inner city. There is a place for white people to work in the black community but, as the Mission Year workers have demonstrated, they have to function in such a way as to lift up rather than put down the work of indigenous people.

> *For those who live in the inner city, enough ministries already exist. The problem is that those who need help from those ministries seldom seek them out.*

Too often, ministries of young white people descend into black communities to do short-term mission work. They are there for a few weeks, behave in a very paternalistic fashion, and then retreat from those communities, leaving a ministry vacuum in their wake. They are almost like teams engaged in guerrilla warfare—they invade and then disappear. Black communities need long-term commitments, lived out in such a way as to lend support and in no way compete.

The young people in the Mission Year program are taught over and over again the Franciscan belief that God uses people sacramentally. St. Francis meant that God uses ordinary people we encounter on life's journeys as a means of grace. If we are ready to receive a stranger, Jesus comes to that stranger through a Christian who is open to receive him or her. We tell young people, "Don't simply look *at* people, look *into* people. Connect with them spiritually. Enter into such intimacy that you feel your way into their souls." As white people connect with black people in their neighborhoods in such a way, an intimacy is created that transcends racial barriers.

It has been amazing over the last few years to see how many of the volunteers choose to remain in the neighborhoods where they served in the missionary program. What is even more surprising is how many report that they have taken a room with one of the neighbors with whom they became especially close during the year of their urban residence. Now they find it easy to live in the same house, to eat at the same table, to participate in the lives of the people. Through the lives of people, who just a year earlier posed a significant threat, racial reconciliation takes place.

> "Don't simply look at people, but look into people. Connect with them spiritually. Enter into such intimacy that you feel your way into their souls."

A contemplative spirituality can lead to such intimacy. Spiritual people sense Christ in others, and must embrace others regardless of racial identity. In so doing, Christians sense that they are embracing their Lord in the process. This is the kind of intimacy that is at the heart of Christianity—the source of ultimate freedom from racism.

Questions
for Reflection

As noted from the outset, racism today is more often expressed in subtle and covert ways rather than blatant racist behaviors such as derogatory language or illegal discriminatory acts. Because of the shame that has become associated with racism in our time, it has become difficult for white people to acknowledge their participation in modern racist behaviors and attitudes, and for people of color to confront their own internalized racism to themselves, their peer groups, and to one another. For this reason, some groups may find it difficult to discuss together some of the ideas in this book or the following questions. They will need to discern for themselves the comfort and trust level they have with one another in order to talk honestly about their experiences of and feelings about racism. But the foundation for racial reconciliation in church and society lies in honest self-appraisal and confession of one's participation in oppressive structures and behaviors. Therefore, we encourage groups who wish to grapple with these issues to do so with the guidance from books such as *Difficult Conversations: Taking Risks, Acting with Integrity* by Katie Day. This excellent, small book helps congregations "give themselves permission" to talk about controversial issues, and specifically looks at racism and multiculturalism as one of those "difficult conversations." Preparing your discussion group by working through some trust and covenanting exercises can lead to more fruitful discussion and facilitate action for positive change.

Chapter 1: What Is Racism?

1. (a) How aware are you of the history of civil rights in the United States? (b) What impressions do you have of the leaders of these movements? (c) Have you personally participated in any civil rights organizations, marches, or other activities related to issues of racial equality?

2. (a) Reflect on any overt or "old-fashioned" racist behaviors that you have witnessed, been the victim of, or personally exhibited. Share these according to the trust level that has been established in your group. How did you or others respond to these behaviors when they occurred? (b) If these behaviors occurred some time ago (say, during childhood), how has time changed your understanding or perception of them? (c) How do you feel or respond now when you witness such behaviors?

3. Consider the five behaviors of modern racism listed on p. 4. (a) Have you witnessed or has someone you know experienced any of these behaviors in your workplace? Your home or family? Your community (or other social circles)? Your church? (b) Do you recognize any times that you yourself have exhibited any of these behaviors? (c) Is this new information for you, or have you had to confront these behaviors in the past? (d) What was your response when you witnessed or experienced this behavior, or recognized this behavior in yourself? (e) Are there other subtle expressions of modern racism not listed here that you have witnessed or experienced?

4. (a) Consider the five behaviors of internalized racism on p. 6. Have you witnessed or has someone you know experienced any of these behaviors in your workplace? Your home or family? Your community (or other social circles)? Your church? (b) Do you recognize any times that you or someone you know has exhibited any of these behaviors? (c) Is this new information for you, or have you had to confront

these behaviors in the past? (d) What was your response
when you witnessed this behavior or recognized this behavior in yourself? (e) Are there other subtle expressions of
internalized racism not listed here that you have witnessed
or experienced?

5. (a) When you reflect on the imbeddedness of racism in American society, do you feel discouraged, resigned, or hopeful? Why?
(b) How have you participated in what Melvin Peters calls the
"politics of resignation" (i.e., what coping strategies—such as
participation in racial affinity groups—have you adopted to
deal with a sense of the unlikelihood that racial conditions will
change in your lifetime?)? (c) Besides participating in this study
group, what are the other ways that you have been able to act
out of a sense of hopefulness and exercised the "politics of education"?

Chapter 2: Christianity and Racism

1. Read Galatians 3:28 to yourself silently or have one person
read it aloud slowly while others in the group close their eyes
and listen. Reflect on Paul's words for a few minutes. (a) Do
you hear anything new in this verse that you have not heard
before? (b) Has your understanding of this verse been more of
a sense of convenient alliances or of a description of true unity
in Christ grounded in baptism? (c) What sorts of convenient
alliances do you see in the life of the church today?

2. Think about the racial make-up of your congregation. (a) Does
Martin Luther King Jr.'s statement about 10 AM on Sunday
morning being the most segregated hour in North America ring
true in your church? (b) How does the racial make-up of your
worshiping community compare to that in other your other life
situations—workplace, social groups, clubs, etc.?

3. Reflect on the authors' assertion that the black church may
be understood under a rubric of "Christ versus culture"—as

needing a common enemy such as racism for the formation of its identity. (a) Based on your own experience and what you have read so far, do you feel that this is a correct view? Why or why not? (b) What sorts of identity issues do you think afflict Christian churches today? (c) Do you think that black and white churches have different identity issues, or are they similar?

4. (a) Think about the pictures of Jesus that decorate the church you currently attend, and of other churches that you have been a part. How have they depicted Jesus? As black? As white? Of undistinguishable racial identity? (b) What pictures have most influenced your current images of Jesus? (c) How do you feel when you see nontraditional pictures of Jesus that depict him as a symbol of other cultures or races? (d) In what ways do you think churches continue to represent God or Jesus in culturally privileged ways?

5. Nelson Mandela has said that he would not have become the person he is had it not been for Christian missionaries in South Africa. Yet that history of missions in Africa and elsewhere is marked by both conversion and violence, and is one source for the church enslavement that is the theme of this book. (a) When you consider that ambiguous history of Christian missions, how do you feel about ongoing missionizing in second- and third-world countries? (b) Have your views on mission work changed over the years? If so, how?

Chapter 3: Ongoing Legacies of Racism

1. (a) Do you think Daniel Moynihan's advocacy of a governmental policy of "benign neglect" toward black families has had ongoing effects on the African American community? (b) If so, do you think this effect has been positive or negative?

2. (a) Do you sense that white people tend to talk differently amongst themselves about black people than when they are

in mixed situations? (b) Is the same true of how black people talk about white people? (c) Do white people lack honesty and truth-telling when it comes to racial issues? (d) What sorts of barriers have you experienced in your congregation in discussing race and racism? (e) Do you sense discomfort and dismissiveness when it comes to racial issues, or are people able to speak openly and honestly with one another about race?

3. (a) How do you respond to Stanford Lyman's question regarding whether black slaves, who often portrayed themselves to their masters as lazy or stupid as a survival technique, came to believe that image themselves, and that this may contribute to a legacy of self-defeating behaviors in the African American community?

4. According to the comfort and trust level of your group, share with one another some of the stories and thoughts that you would be otherwise reluctant to discuss when black and white people are together. (a) Do you agree that black people have often failed to take advantage of the opportunities made available to them? (b) If so, what do you believe contributes to this failure?

Chapter 4: Racist Myths and Taboos

1. Reflect on Eldridge Cleaver's assertions about the mind–body dichotomy and how that has influenced Western attitudes toward race. (a) Do you regard black people as being generally physically superior to white people? (b) Do you regard white people as generally intellectually superior to black people? (c) Why?

2. (a) If you are white, have you ever felt intimidated by a black person in a situation where physical aptitude was a key factor, such as a sports situation? (b) If you are black, have you ever felt intimidated by a white person in a situation where intellectual aptitude was a key factor, such as the classroom?

3.   (a) What physical attributes do you admire most in people of ethnic groups other than your own? (b) What physical attributes do you admire least? (c) How do you think those feelings are influenced by Western standards of beauty?

4.   Consider Malcolm X's story about the extremes he went to in order to measure up to a "white" standard of appearance. (a) Do you recognize any sorts of appearance standards today that seem to be race-related? (b) If you are a person of color, have you ever felt pressure to match up to a similar standard? (c) Have you ever done anything to address such cultural pressure that you now regret?

5.   (a) Do you think that there are differences in sexual drives and abilities between black and white people? (b) How do you feel when you see a mixed-race couple? (c) What sorts of race-related sexual fears do you think still influence attitudes and behaviors in American society? (d) What sort of work do you think churches need to do to address effectively the sexual overtones that affect relationships between black people and white people?

Chapter 5: Challenges for White Churches

1.   (a) Do you think there are differences between mainline Protestant churches and Evangelical churches regarding racial reconciliation issues? (b) If so, which do you think are more successful in dealing with these issues constructively?

2.   (a) What behaviors do you see in your own church and/or denomination that may support the continuation of racism in America? (b) Do you think your church or denomination only pays lip service to racial understanding and does little or nothing substantial to promote racial understanding?

3.   (a) Do you agree that white Evangelical churches have become primarily identified with the Republican Party? (b) If so, do

you think this political identification influences racial understanding in positive or negative ways? (c) Do you recognize
any governmental policies or political stances that may have
negative racial implications?

4. (a) Do you believe in the existence of systemic evil? Why or
    why not? (b) Do you think that the idea of systemic evil is
    overplayed or underplayed relative to matters of personal
    morality? (c) Do you agree that the Evangelical church has
    become focused on matters of individualism? (d) Is this true
    as well in mainline Protestant churches? (e) Black churches?

Chapter 6: Challenges for Black Churches

1. (a) What positive aspects do you see to the separation of people
    into mostly black churches or mostly white churches? (b) What
    negative aspects do you see?

2. (a) Have you ever attended worship at a storefront church? If
    so, what were your impressions? (b) How did it differ from
    your usual church experience? (c) Does your church engage
    any storefront churches on any matters of mutual interest or
    offer financial or other forms of support?

3. (a) Have you ever attended worship in a black megachurch or
    seen a media broadcast of a black megachurch event? (b) If so,
    what were your impressions? (c) How did it differ from your
    usual church experience? (d) How do you feel about mega-
    church programs to rebuild decaying urban neighborhoods
    and to create job opportunities for African Americans in those
    communities?

4. (a) Have you ever attended worship in a black mainline
    church? (b) If so, what were your impressions? (c) How did
    it differ from your usual church experience? (d) Has your
    church ever interacted with a black mainline church on issues
    of mutual interest (or, if you are from a black mainline church,

has your church ever interacted with a mostly white church in this manner)? (e) If so, did you experience the sort of lack of black participation noted by the authors? If so, what do you attribute that to?

5. (a) Do you agree that black churches tend to identify with the Democratic Party? Why? (b) If so, what advantages and disadvantages do you see to this identification?

6. (a) To what degree do you think "gay friendly" policies influence the political participation and voting patterns of black Christians? (b) How do you think the battle for gay and lesbian rights differs from the battle for civil rights? (c) How are they similar? (d) Do you think that black Christians tend to play a "we-they" game with gays and lesbians, and have made them the new "out" group? Why or why not?

Chapter 7: A Community of Hope

1. (a) Reflect on the authors' assertion that the West emphasizes self-determination, self-achievement, and self-satisfaction. Do you agree or disagree? (b) If you agree, how do you think this influences your day-to-day behavior and attitudes? (c) Your faith and personal beliefs? (d) Your attitudes toward race?

2. (a) Does your church's theology seem to encourage or discourage a self-understanding of community interdependence? How? (b) Does this conflict with messages that you receive from your family, workplace, media, or other social connections?

3. (a) How do you think your church would change if it embraced a more African understanding of communal salvation? (b) How might this affect your personal attitudes and behavior, particularly with regards to race?

4. (a) Do you think that African understandings of creation, community, and ancestral connections enhance, compliment,

or conflict with traditional Christian understandings of these topics? How?

Chapter 8: A Commitment to Justice

1. (a) What barriers in American society do you see to embracing a pastoral theology of forgiveness and reconciliation as espoused by Archbishop Desmond Tutu? (b) Do you think his *Ubunu* theology conflicts with or compliments your church's understanding of forgiveness? How?

2. (a) Is your personal perspective on justice of a more retributive nature or do you agree with the restorative approach? Why? (b) How do you think the American justice system would change if it embraced more restorative processes? (c) Would this be good or bad? Why?

3. (a) Do you think that restorative justice processes would be useful for discussing issues of racism and discrimination in churches and in public forums? Why or why not? (b) What barriers in American society do you see to embracing restorative justice processes?

Chapter 9: A Spirituality of Healing

1. Reflect on your own personal theological beliefs. (a) What themes do you see as most prominent in your belief system? (b) What place does justice play in your theological convictions? (c) What about suffering?

2. Reflect on Howard Thurman's comments on suffering in the Christian life. (a) How are his ideas similar to or different from your own understandings? (b) Do you agree that suffering has the power to create community? (c) If so, where have you experienced or witnessed this personally?

3. Do you sense comfort or discomfort in your church with regard to talking about death? (b) Is conversation on death

focused on what happens in the afterlife, or the impact of the reality of death on the community here on Earth? (c) What difference does this make in the context of racism?

4. (a) Discuss together your understandings of the meaning of baptism. (b) What barriers in church and society do you see to people embracing baptism as the primary basis for their identity? (c) How might the church change if it embraced this identity more fully? (d) What would need to change in the church for this to happen?

Chapter 10: A Practice of Contemplation

1. (a) What is your understanding of the place of prayer in the Christian life? (b) Does your church encourage prayer as the vocation of all Christians, or is praying, especially in public, implied to be the work of "professionals"?

2. (a) Have you ever participated in contemplative prayer, either individually or in a group setting? If so, share your experience of that with the group. (b) Has contemplative prayer changed or shaped your personal faith in any way? How?

3. (a) Do you think intentionally embracing mystical or contemplative spirituality could change personal attitudes toward race? Why or why not? (b) If so, how?

4. (a) Have you ever sensed that God was asking you to look at another person, in particular a person of another race, differently? (b) If so, did you sense that you were looking at that person through the eyes of Jesus, or that God had transformed your attitude?

5. (a) Do you think your personal spirituality is more *head, heart, kingdom,* or *mystical*? (b) How does that influence how you think about race and being a community of racial reconciliation?

Chapter 11: A Church of Reconciliation

1. (a) Have you ever been led in worship by a black person, either in a white or black church? (b) If so, how did that differ from your usual church experience?

2. (a) Have you ever considered joining a black church? (b) What would be the barriers to your doing so or considering that as an option?

3. (a) Reflect on the social programs that your church operates. Do you think these programs are genuinely helpful to persons in need, or are they patronizing or even damaging to the participants? Why?

4. (a) Discuss together the difference between charity work and community service. What pluses and minuses do you see to each approach?

5. Reflect on Valerie Batts's four levels of racism and then consider the racial make-up of your congregation and your welcoming policies to persons of color. (a) Do you see racism operating on any or all of these levels in your congregation? (b) What about your workplace or other social groups?

6. (a) What factors make it hard to speak the truth in love to one another about racial issues? (b) Do you find it easier to point out shortcomings on racial attitudes to persons of your own race or to persons of another race?

Resources

The list of print, film/video, online, and organizational resources listed below is a small selection from the numerous resources available, but they represent some that we will believe will be most helpful to our readers. We are indebted to the outstanding bibliography from Sheryl A. Kujawa-Holbrook's *A House of Prayer for All Peoples* (listed below) for many of the listings, and we recommend her book for those looking for further resources.

Books and Articles

Barndt, Joseph. *Dismantling Racism: The Continuing Challenge to White America*. Minneapolis: Augsburg Books, 1991. Widely used among antiracism trainers, this is an important fundamental work for churches and other communities.

Battle, Michael. *Reconciliation: The Ubuntu Theology of Desmond Tutu*. Cleveland: The Pilgrim Press, 1997. Explains in more detail the work and theology of Desmond Tutu, which was briefly described in chapter 7.

Batts, Valerie. *Modern Racism: New Melody for the Same Old Tunes*. Cambridge, Mass.: Episcopal Divinity School Occasional Papers, 1998. Offers a model for identifying

and changing modern racism. Available at http://www.
episdivschool.edu.

Campolo, Tony, with stories by Bruce Main. *Revolution and
Renewal: How Churches Are Saving Our Cities*. Louisville,
Ky.: Westminister John Knox, 2000. Argues that Christian
churches need to take the lead not only in getting involved
with urban schools and prisons, but also in actively luring
business development to decaying inner-city communities.

Cone, James A. "Black Theology in American Religion," *Theology
Today* 43, no. 1 (April 1986): 7. A key article by the dean of
black theology in the United States. Succinctly lays out the
basic themes of black theology and analyzes their political
significance.

Day, Kate. *Difficult Conversations: Taking Risks, Acting with
Integrity*. Bethesda, Md.: The Alban Institute, 2001.

DeYoung, Curtiss Paul, et al. *United by Faith: The Multiracial
Congregation as an Answer to the Problem of Race*. New York:
Oxford University Press, 2002. Based on a major research
project, DeYoung and his co-authors argue that multiracial
congregations are a potentially powerful force for eradicating
racism in modern society. DeYoung is a powerful voice
among white Evangelicals on antiracism issues. His other
books, including *Reconciliation: Our Greatest Challenge—Our
Greatest Hope* (Valley Forge, Pa.: Judson Press, 1997), are also
highly recommended.

Emerson, Michael O., and Christian Smith. *Divided by Faith:
Evangelical Religion and the Problem of Race in America*. New
York: Oxford University Press, 2000. In addition to showing
how white Evangelicals have helped to perpetuate the racism
they publicly oppose, the book also shows the relationship
between religion and racism.

Felder, Cain Hope. *Race, Racism, and the Biblical Narratives.* Prisms. Minneapolis: Fortress Press, 2002. A small book that shows how the Bible has been used to trivialize African contributions and demean and enslave black people.

Kujawa-Holbrook, Sheryl A. *A House of Prayer for All Peoples: Congregations Building Multiracial Community.* Bethesda, Md.: The Alban Institute, 2002. A powerful study of seven mainline Protestant congregations that have deliberately engaged the challenge to move beyond racism and form multiracial faith communities. In addition to its fine bibliography, it also offers ideas on talking about race and racism, a glossary of terms, and a list of characteristics of healthy multiracial congregations.

Thurman, Howard. *A Strange Freedom: The Best of Howard Thurman on Religious Experience and Public Life*, ed. Walter Earl Fluker and Catherine Tumber (Boston: Beacon Press, 1998). A compelling collection of the African American mystical theologian's key works.

Tutu, Desmond. *No Future Without Forgiveness.* New York: Random House, 1999. Written from his perspective of ministry in South Africa, this book offers a bold spirituality that takes seriously the reality of oppression and the idealism of reconciliation.

West, Cornel. *Race Matters.* Boston: Beacon Press, 1992. An important resource that explores the crisis of black leadership in America and argues that racism breaks down the democratic order.

Films and Videos

Black Is . . . Black Ain't. Produced and directed by Marlon Riggs. 87 min. 1995. Discussion by bell hooks, Cornel West, and others of the diversity of black identities. Study guide included. Available from the Western States Consortium, P.O. Box 40305, Portland, OR 97240. Web site: http://www. westernstatescenter.org.

Let the Church Say Amen! Produced and directed by David Petersen. 87 min. 2003. A video portrait of a storefront church, the World Missions for Christ Church, located in the Shaw neighborhood of inner-city Washington, D.C. Available from Film Movement at http://www.filmmovement.com.

Lift Every Voice: The Bible in an Age of Diversity. Produced by Seraphim Communications. 2 tapes. 128 min. 1994. A five-part video Bible study on the dynamics of a diverse society featuring Cain Hope Felder and Tony Campolo. Available from Seraphim Communications, 1568 Eustis St., St. Paul, MN 55108. Web site: http://www.scracomm.com.

Organizations and Web Sites

Congress of National Black Churches (CNBC). 1225 I Street NW, Washington, DC 20005. Web site: http://www.cnbc. org. An ecumenical coalition of eight historically black denominations.

Evangelical Association for the Promotion of Education (EAPE). P.O. Box 2738, St. Davids, PA 19087. Web site: http://www. tonycampolo.org/eape.shtml. An organization founded by Tony Campolo that has developed and nurtured elementary and secondary schools, universities, adult and child literacy centers, tutoring programs, orphanages, AIDS hospices, urban youth ministries, summer camps, and long-term Christian service programs in Haiti, the Dominican Republic, Africa, Canada, and throughout the USA.

Mission Year. 2520 S. Western Avenue #304, Chicago, IL 60608. Web site: http://www.missionyear.org. Described in detail in chapter 11, this organization sponsors teams of six young people in Oakland, Chicago, Atlanta, and Philadelphia who live, volunteer, and worship in an inner-city community for one year, serving people in the name of Jesus.

Project Change. P.O. Box 29919, San Francisco, CA 94129. Web site: http://www.projectchange.org. An organization working to strengthen the antiracism infrastructure. They have numerous helpful online resources and publications, including the AntiRacism.Net Web site (http://www. antiracismnet.org), and the *Anti-Racism Resource Guide*, available for download from http://www.projectchange.org/ publications/guidetext.pdf

Southern Poverty Law Center. 400 Washington Ave., Montgomery, AL 36104. Web site: http://www.splcenter. org. An organization that battles hate, intolerance, and discrimination through education and litigation. They have numerous print, video, and online resources available through their Teaching Tolerance Web site, http://www. tolerance.org.

Chapter 1: What Is Racism?

1. Valerie Batts, "Is Reconciliation Possible? Lessons from Combating 'Modern Racism,'" in *Waging Reconciliation: God's Mission in a Time of Globalization and Crisis*, ed. Ian T. Douglas (New York: Church Publishing, 2002), chap. 2.

2. Ibid.

3. Melvin Peters, Private Communication, Duke University.

4. "All Things Bright and Beautiful," text by Cecil Alexander, 1848.

Chapter 2: Christianity and Racism

1. Malcolm X, as told to Alex Haley, *The Autobiography of Malcolm X* (New York: Ballantine, 1973), 222.

2. Albert J. Raboteau, *Slave Religion: The "Invisible Institution" in the Antebellum South* (New York: Oxford University Press, 1980).

3. H. Richard Niebuhr, *Christ and Culture* (New York: Harper & Row, 1951).

4. Charles Villa-Vicencio, *Civil Disobedience and Beyond: Law, Resistance, and Religion in South Africa* (Grand Rapids, Mich.: Eerdmans, 1990).

5. Johann Baptist Metz, *Faith in History and Society: Towards a Practical Fundamental Theology* (London: Burns and Oates, 1980), 88f.

6. James Cone, "Black Theology in American Religion," in *Theology Today* 43(1986): 6–21; 6.

7. W. E. B. DuBois, *The Souls of Black Folk* (Greenwich, Conn.: Fawcett Premier Books, 1968), 16–17.

8. Emile Durkheim, *The Elementary Forms of the Religious Life*, trans. Karen E. Fields (New York: Free Press, 1995).

9. Milton C. Sernett, ed., *Afro-American Religious History: A Documentary Witness* (Durham, N.C.: Duke University Press, 1985), 25.

10. Cone, "Black Theology in American Religion," 7.

Chapter 3: Ongoing Legacies of Racism

1. Daniel P. Moynihan, *The Negro Family: The Case for National Action* (Washington, D.C.: U.S. Department of Labor, 1965).

2. Elliot Liebow, *Talley's Corner* (Boston: Little, Brown, 1967).

3. William Julius Wilson, *The Truly Disadvantaged: The Inner City, the Underclass, and Public Policy* (Chicago: University of Chicago Press, 1987).

4. William Julius Wilson, *When Work Disappears: The World of the New Urban Poor* (New York: Knopf, 1996).

5. Ralph Ellison, *Invisible Man* (New York: Random House, 1952).

6. Shelby Steele, *The Content of Our Character: A New Vision of Race in America* (New York: St. Martin's Press, 1990).

7. Cornel West, *Race Matters* (Boston: Beacon Press, 1993).

Chapter 4: Racist Myths and Taboos

1. Eldridge Cleaver, *Soul on Ice* (New York: McGraw-Hill, 1967).

2. Julius "Dr. J" Erving, radio interview, KYW AM Philadelphia, February 20, 1988.

3. Cornel West, *Race Matters* (Boston: Beacon Press, 1993).

4. John Dollard, *Caste and Class in a Southern Town* (Madison: University of Wisconsin Press, 1989).

5. Harper Lee, *To Kill a Mockingbird* (New York: Harper & Row, 1960).

Chapter 5: Challenges for White Churches

1. Sheryl A. Kujawa-Holbrook, *A House of Prayer for All Peoples: Congregations Creating Multiracial Community* (Bethesda, Md.: The Alban Institute, 2002).

2. Hendrik Berkhof, *Christ and the Powers*, ed. and trans. John Howard Yoder (Scottdale, Pa.: Herald Press, 1977).

3. William Stringfellow, *An Ethic for Christians and Other Aliens in a Strange Land* (Waco, Tex.: Word, 1973).

Chapter 6: Challenges for Black Churches

1. For an excellent portrait of a "typical" black storefront church and the people it serves, see the documentary *Let the Church Say Amen* by David Petersen (2003), which highlights one such church in Washington, D.C.

2. For a recent discussion of this widening gap, see Dale P. Andrews, *Practical Theology for Black Churches: Bridging Black Theology and African American Folk Religion* (Louisville: Westminster John Knox, 2002).

3. Philip Jenkins, *The Next Christendom: The Coming of Global Christianity* (New York: Oxford University Press, 2003).

Chapter 7: A Community of Hope

1. Desmond Tutu, "Postscript" to "To Be Human Is to Be Free," *The Wisdom of Desmond Tutu* (Oxford: Lion, 1998), 317.

2. Desmond Tutu, Addresses and Speeches, "What Jesus Means to Me," Durban University, August 6-7, 1981.

3. Ibid.

4. See Michael Battle, *Reconciliation: The Ubuntu Theology of Desmond Tutu*, (Cleveland: Pilgrim, 1997).

5. A well-known African philosopher and theologian, John Mbiti, agrees. See John S. Mbiti, *African Religions and Philosophy* (London: Heinemann, 1969), 39–41.

6. Ibid.

7. J. S. Pobee, *Toward an African Theology* (Nashville: Abingdon, 1979), 47.

8. Mbiti, *African Religions*, 57.

9. Ibid., 81.

Chapter 8: A Commitment to Justice

1. Quoted in David Beresford, "Fisher of Men, Seeker of Truth," *Johannesburg Mail & Guardian*, December 19, 1997.

2. See Desmond Tutu, *No Future without Forgiveness* (New York: Doubleday, 1999).

3. Ibid.

4. From a sermon preached by Tutu at St. Philip's Episcopal Church, Washington D.C., Christmas 1984.

5. Desmond Tutu, quoted in *Prayers for Peace*, Archbishop Robert Runcie and Cardinal Basil Hume, eds. (London: SPCK, 1987), 41.

6. Desmond Tutu, "The Nature and Value of Theology," unpublished paper.

7. Marian Liebmann, "Restorative Justice—An Overview," from *Restorative Justice—What's It All About?* ed. Churches' Criminal Justice

Forum (2001), a network of Churches Together in Britain and Ireland (CTBI), available from CTBI's Web site http://www.ctbi.org.uk/chsoc/Restorative%20Justice.doc, 6–7.

8. John Braithwaite, stated in Jean Wynne, "Restorative Justice in the Criminal Justice System," in *Restorative Justice—What's It All About?* 26.

9. Annette Hinton, "Restorative Justice in a Christian Context," in *Restorative Justice—What's It All About?* 16.

Chapter 9: A Spirituality of Healing

1. James Cone, "Black Theology in American Religion," *Theology Today* 43, no. 1 (April 1986): 7.

2. Ibid., 9; Cone quotes C. G. Woodson, ed., *The Works of Francis J. Grimke, vol. 1* (Washington, D.C.: Associated Publishers, 1942), 354.

3. "Suffering," in Howard Thurman, *A Strange Freedom: The Best of Howard Thurman on Religious Experience and Public Life,* ed. Walter Earl Fluker and Catherine Tumber (Boston: Beacon Press, 1998). Page numbers for selections from this title are cited in the text.

4. "Excerpt from *The Luminous Darkness* (1965)," in Fluker and Tumber, eds., *A Strange Freedom,* 247–48.

5. Ibid., 246.

6. Geoffrey Wainwright, *Doxology: The Praise of God in Worship, Doctrine, and Life: A Systematic Theology* (New York: Oxford University Press, 1980), 365.

7. Josiah Young, *Black and African Theologies: Siblings or Distant Cousins?* (Maryknoll, N.Y.: Orbis Books, 1986).

8. Wainwright, *Doxology,* 365.

9. Lamin Sanneh, *Translating the Message: The Missionary Impact on Culture* (Maryknoll, N.Y.: Orbis Books, 1989).

10. Thurman, *The Luminous Darkness,* 95.

11. Maggie Ross, *Pillars of Flame: Power, Priesthood, and Spiritual Maturity* (New York: HarperCollins, 1988), 171.

12. Stanley Hauerwas, *The Peaceable Kingdom: A Primer on Christian Ethics* (Notre Dame, Ind.: University of Notre Dame Press, 1984), 21.

Chapter 10: A Practice of Contemplation

1. See, however, the enlightening work of Barbara A. Holmes, *Joy Unspeakable: Contemplative Practices of the Black Church* (Minneapolis: Fortress Press, 2004).

2. Corinne Ware, *Discover Your Spiritual Type: A Guide to Individual and Congregational Growth* (Bethesda, Md.: The Alban Institute, 1995).

Chapter 11: A Church of Reconciliation

1. Sonia Nieto, foreword to *Integrating Service Learning and Multicultural Education in Colleges and Universities*, ed. Carolyn O'Grady (Mahwah, N.J.: Lawrence Erlbaum, 2000), ix.

2. Parker Palmer, "Community, Conflict and Ways of Knowing: Ways to Deepen Our Educational Agenda," in *Combining Service and Learning: A Resource Book for Community and Public Service*, vol. 1, J. C. Kendal & Associates, ed. (Raleigh, N.C.: National Society for Internships and Experiential Education, 1990), 106.

3. R. A. Rhoads, *Community Service and Higher Learning: Explorations of the Caring Self* (Albany, N.Y.: State University of New York Press, 1997), 208.

4. Nieto, foreword to *Integrating Service Learning*, xi.

5. "Is Reconciliation Possible? Lessons from Combating 'Modern Racism,'" in *Waging Reconciliation: God's Mission in a Time of Globalization and Crisis*, ed. Ian Douglas (New York: Church Publishing Inc., 2002), 35–77.

6. Cornel West, *Race Matters* (Boston: Beacon Press, 1993).